AMERICAN INDIAN LIVES

Turtle Lung Woman's Granddaughter

Delphine Red Shirt

University of Nebraska Press, Lincoln and London

Manufactured in the
United States of America
⊗
First Nebraska paperback
printing: 2003
Library of Congress
Cataloging-in-Publication
Data
Red Shirt, Delphine, 1957–
Turtle Lung Woman's
granddaughter / Delphine
Red Shirt   p.   cm. –
(American Indian lives)
ISBN 0-8032-3947-5
(cl. : alk. paper)
ISBN 0-8032-8996-0
(pa. : alk. paper)
1. Lone Woman.
2. Turtle Lung Woman.
3. Red Shirt, Delphine,
1957–
4. Teton women –
Biography.
5. Teton women – Social
life and customs.
6. Pine Ridge Indian
Reservation (S.D.) –
History.
7. Pine Ridge Indian
Reservation (S.D.) – Social
life and customs.
I. Title: Keglezela Cagu
Win's granddaughter.
II. Title. III. Series.
E99.T34 R339 2002
978.3'66—dc21
2001037661

Hená eháni wabláke
eháni hená
Thatéya ki ék'aš wašté
táku echúpikte
hená iyóptepteya
Thatéya hé tha'í
wóchekiye na táku ki
Ho lehál
áta otúyachi
tuktógna tha'íšni
uk'úyap s'eleca

These things
I saw
long ago
when
even the wind blowing
was good
In all things
the people did
the wind
made itself known
In prayer
in all things
it was good
Now it seems
we have no purpose
no reason
no direction
We are lost

Lone Woman
(Wíya Išnála),
November 1997

This book is dedicated in memory of

Kheglézela Chaǧúwį   Wíyą Išnála
1851–1935   1920–1999

Contents

PART 3:
Death

Acknowledgments

I am grateful to Frances Densmore for recording all the old Lakota songs I have included in each chapter. The songs are prayers spoken with grateful hearts, the way the people lived long ago.

I am grateful for the material collected by James R. Walker and made available through the Colorado Historical Society. I am grateful for the Lakota voice of George (Long Knife) Sword, which is present in the material collected by Walker. I am grateful for the documents retained by the Colorado Historical Society that are written in the Lakota language, the language of my true self. Some of these materials are incorporated in this book.

I am grateful to the Endangered Language Fund, Department of Linguistics, at Yale University. I am thankful for their decision to support this important project to record my mother's story. With their assistance I was able to work to preserve the Lakota language as it was spoken by my mother's generation. Lakota words are written in the standard Lakota orthography used by the University of Nebraska Press (see "Orthographic Key"); the words as spoken and written reflect the masculine or feminine voice of the speaker. The chapter-opening songs are all in the masculine voice.

I honor my mother, Wíyą Išnála, for choosing to share her story. I am grateful for her willingness to tell it in her first language and to trust me to translate it for her. "Miyé átayela, owáglake," she insisted throughout the two years it took us to record her story, "Of my own accord, I tell my life story."

Through this writing I honor the memory of my great-grandmother, Turtle Lung Woman. "Wíyą wašté hécha," she was a good strong woman. I am grateful to my grandmother for teaching my mother the Lakota ways.

I am forever indebted to Richard Harding Shaw for the unflagging support and admiration he continues to bestow upon me, through all my doubts. I am grateful to Justin Hill Shaw, my son, for his belief in the old ways. I feel fortunate to have two beautiful daughters, Chąkú Waštéwį, or Woman of a Good Road (Way), and Ȟokáwį, or Badger Woman, Megan and Kirsten. They are Turtle Lung Woman's great-great-granddaughters.

I am indebted to Griffin Laengle for her patience and commitment to my family. I would not have found the time to continue my work without her presence.

I wish to thank Charlotte Currier, Catherine Stock-Lefeber, Alan Trachtenberg, and Keith Rabin for agreeing to read the manuscript for me.

Orthographic and Pronunciation Key

Because many diverse systems have been used to write Dakota and Lakota, Lakota words and phrases used throughout this volume have been systematically retranscribed to conform to the orthography of Rood and Taylor (1996). Phonemic spellings are used throughout and are complemented by the pronunciation guide below. Although phonemic spellings are normally indicated with italic type, the publisher has not applied this linguistic convention. Lakota terms and phrases, excluding proper nouns, are indicated with quotation marks. Those terms used repeatedly are run in with the English text. Special symbols are as follows:

ą   nasalized "a," pronounced as "an" in the French word "enfant"

c   pronounced as "ch" in "watch"

ǧ   pronounced as a guttural "r," as in the French pronunciation of "Paris"

h   indicates aspiration when following a consonant; thus, for example, the sequence "th" in Lakota is pronounced strongly as "t" in "toe," and not as "th" in "thin"

ȟ   pronounced as "ch" in the German composer's name "Bach"

į   nasalized "i," pronounced as "in" in the French word "vin"

š   pronounced as "sh" in "ship"

ų   nasalized "u," pronounced as the French word "un"

ž   pronounced as the second "g" in "garage"

'   glottal stop, as in "oh-oh!"

Introduction

My mother told me a story when I began to record her. She told me about Winúȟcala (Old Woman) Standing Soldier, a woman who lived near where my mother came to draw water from a hand pump each day. They both lived in a small town in Nebraska near the reservation.

My mother stopped in each day to see her. She would say hello and visit with her. She even took time to sweep her floors. Sometimes she would start soup in a pot for her. The old woman seemed to appreciate everything my mother did for her.

She was a relative, although not directly related to my mother. She was my father's "thuwí," his aunt. She was the mother of Andrew Standing Soldier, who later in his life became known as an artist who depicted life among the Lakota. My father's grandmother and Andrew's grandmother were sisters. They were descendants of a man named Chief Lone Elk from the Brulé side of our family. Chief Lone Elk was the son-in-law of Battiste Good, also a Brulé, who kept an important winter count for our people.

My mother told me that Winúȟcala Standing Soldier was alone when she came to see her. She used to tell my mother, "Kiktápi na owížža kį onášloka na iyápi," referring to her grandchildren, "They shed their bedcovers and are gone." The old woman seemed lonely. My mother made it a point to visit the old woman, who perhaps reminded her of her grandmother, Turtle Lung Woman.

Winúȟcala Standing Soldier looked forward to her visits. One day my mother stopped going because she was busy with her life. When she resumed her visits a few days later, Old Woman Standing Soldier was happy beyond words. "Where have you been?" she asked. "I have been waiting for you." My mother realized then how much her visits meant to the old woman. After that, she tried not to miss a visit again.

"When I came back that time after I was gone for a few days, the old woman told me that she had nothing in the world to give me. Nothing material, that is. The one thing she would give me is a word I would never forget," my mother told me. " 'Ayáwašte mak'ú.' She gave me her blessing. That was what she gave me, that old woman. I know she gave it to me, because I have felt it. After her death, I felt it. Her blessing remained with me."

My mother finished the story and looked into her wide and deep lap. She had been eating grapes that were set in her lap as if they were put upon a neatly set table. She sat like that, as far back as I can remember, with her food in her lap as she ate. She especially liked fresh fruit for a snack.

We were driving south toward the Rosebud Reservation in western South Dakota on a cloudy August day. The flat road was empty on that Monday morning. I was driving south on State Highway 63, southwest of Eagle Butte. It was then that I began to record her story on tape, later translating it from the Lakota language.

On that quiet morning as she spoke, she paused. "Lakhóta chažé ki hé . . ." she said, telling me the Lakota names of my relatives. All of a sudden, as she paused, an eagle that had been hovering over us dove down, and its wing hit the left side of the car. The great bird rose again and flew away. After the shock of feeling and hearing its wing hit the car on my side, I looked again, but it was gone. You can hear the sound of its wing hitting the car on the tape in the recording we made that morning.

"Wi . . . o," my mother said. "Weee," the way older Lakota women express surprise, and "oh," softly like she felt the bird's wing hitting her. "Eyá wówaglake ki icúha, eyá, wablí wa ukíyoȟpaya gláȟci eyá. Táku wašté é . . . léchi gláȟci eyá," she said, "As I was speaking, an eagle came down very close to us. There will be good . . . it came so near." She saw it as a sign. She remained quiet and reflective.

I stayed on the road to Midland, driving almost a straight line south, crossing over State Highway 34, which heads east to Pierre, the state capitol. After Highway 63 crossed Highway 34, it turned into U.S. Route 14. Highway 34 continued in a straight line to the west. It passed near Bad River. Route 14 took us to the small town of Midland. Here the land is flat and endless. The grass is dull and yellow, turning brown near the earth. We stopped for lunch in Midland, where we bought grilled cheese sandwiches to go. The waitress put them into a brown paper bag and we continued driving south.

Across Interstate 90, Highway 63 became a lesser-known road. It became a gravel road. The land, as we drove south, became rolling hills, undulating west toward the Ȟé Sápa, or Black Hills, in the westernmost part of the state. The Black Hills are forests of yellow pine. Their highest peak rises 7,242 feet above the plains.

Where we were the land was rolling hills. As we drove farther south, I could see the Ȟé Šíca, or Badlands, jutting out between the prairie and the Black Hills. The Ȟé Šíca are barren hills, buttes, and ridges. They were formed by erosion, carved out by water that, over time, ran rapidly off the slopes, creating a barren landscape. That day, as we drove south, they seemed far away.

We drove about thirty miles without seeing another car, the road dipping down into gullies. We crossed the White River near Norris. We continued south to Parmelee, where my father was born. There I saw chokecherry and wild plum trees where a small tributary of the White River meandered onto the reservation. I wanted to stop and pick the ripe chokecherries the way we used to when I was a child and we were on our way to visit relatives near Parmelee. We did not stop but continued south.

When we passed the small town of Parmelee, my mother spoke to me. I thought she had been napping. She had been quiet and reflective. "Míza chic'ú," she said, "I give you what Winúȟcala Standing Soldier gave to me." She continued eating her grapes and I continued driving. We did not discuss what she had just said. It was not necessary to say anything else.

It occurred to me later that my mother had concerned herself with giving me something in return for recording her story. Now I realize that as her child I saw myself only in that role. She, on the other hand, saw me as the adult I had become. While I was not able to separate myself from her, she saw me as the person I had become.

The time it has taken to tell her story, the effort I have put into the translations, the dreams I have had in that process have made me realize how much I am my mother's daughter. She honored me by trusting me to tell her story. She brought joy into the life of an old woman who gave her a blessing. I brought joy into my mother's life by having her relive all the good that was in her life. I am glad I was able to do it for her.

What follows is her story, told in her words.

PART 1

Turtle Lung Woman
(Kheglézela Chaǧúwį)

Watch Your Horse

Khạǧí wicháša kị	Crow man
šúkawakhạ awáglaka po	watch your horses
šúka wamánụ s'a	a horse thief
miyé yelo	I am called

Beading by Moonlight

In the life of the Lakota "oyáte," the Lakota people, before 1868, the "oyáte" lived a certain way. "Hehą́ makhóche ki̧, yąké ki̧ héchųs'e yąké eš tąyą́ wichóni," back then, the land was as it is now, but the people lived a different way. They lived content and pleased with everything around them. They were grateful for everything they had.

It was a time when our people called themselves "ikcé wichá̠ša," or "common man," and lived a certain way. My grandmother Kheglézela Chağúwi̧, Turtle Lung Woman, was a young woman back then. She lived a certain way. The wife of a man with many wives, she was the favored one, the one who sat in the honored place in her tipi, and while the others carried wood, she made moccasins. So it was she sat in the moonlight one night making "hąpíkceka," "common shoes" or moccasins, for her husband, Ité Si̧yą́khiya, Paints His Face with Clay, who was going to war.

She sat singing a song as she made hąpíkceka for him. She sang a song about Ité Si̧yą́khiya, Paints His Face with Clay, going to war: "Zuyá iyáyi̧kte, ehápi k'ų, hé wa̠štéwalake, iyótiyewakiye." The words say, "He is going to war, you have said. He whom I cherish, I shall see hard times."

The Lakota word "zuyá" means "war." We were always at war with the Khağí wichá̠ša, or Crow men. The word "khağí" means "crow." It is the name of the bird, the crow, whose tongue when split it speaks.

The Khağí wichá̠ša "ahíwichaktepi," we say, "they came to kill." When they did, "thókic'ų," we say, "we took revenge" for any killing they did. It seemed like a vicious cycle, they came to kill and we went to strike back. Sometimes they came to take horses and we went to take them back. An old song goes like this:

"Khǧí wicháša kį šúkawakhą awáglaka po, šúka wamánų s'a miyé yelo." This song says, "Crow man, watch your horses, horse stealer, that is who I am." They even took women and children. The Khǧí wicháša was our mortal enemy. He came among us to take our horses or our scalps.

It was one of these times when my grandfather went to war. He went against the Khǧí wicháša. My grandmother Turtle Lung Woman sat under a full moon and made beaded moccasins for him. The full moon we call "hąwí," or "night sun." She preferred it, saying she grew stronger when it was the brightest. Perhaps so the way the men felt as they prepared for war.

"Ápa kį iyécha," she told me, "Its light was as bright as day." She could see well enough to sew. She sat outdoors at night on a piece of soft buckskin. Her long dark hair was neatly braided. A small woman, dressed in trader's cloth and blue leggings with leather moccasins, she sat hunched over her work. She was intent on finishing before daybreak, when Ité Sįyákhiya would leave for war.

She made hąpíkceka. She measured her husband's foot and set out a pattern to sew from. She cut tanned buckskin, folded it with the outer side in, and used an awl to punch holes for sewing. She used buffalo sinew and a bone needle as she pulled each stitch carefully through the holes. She could feel a callus on the heel of her right hand. She worked patiently with the awl, bone needle, and sinew thread. She sewed carefully, flattening out the seams so her husband would not feel any discomfort when he wore his moccasins. They might be the only things he wore into battle that day.

She thought about her husband, Ité Sįyákhiya, a "zuyá wicháša," a warrior. Sometimes he left for a long time when he went to war. She wanted to make sure he had enough moccasins with him. This time he wanted four pairs to take with him. She had started making them earlier that day but had not finished so she had to work by moonlight.

He asked her to go as a "moccasin carrier," a member of the group going to war, but she declined. A moccasin carrier was a brave woman who risked becoming a captive. She could not bear the thought of living with a different

6

oyáte. She thought of the Khąǧí wichášạ and living as a captive among them. She dreaded seeing the black painted face of the Khąǧí wichášạ, who painted his face this way to signify that he had killed many Lakotas.

She knew the other tribes who were our enemies. We fought them when they entered our territory, "Lakhóta ektá hiyúpi hátạ," when they came among us. We fought the people we called "Pheží wokhéya othí kị," meaning "grass house dwellers," the Shoshones, and those we called "Wichášạ Yúta," meaning "man eater," the Utes, whom we knew were cannibalistic. The tribe we considered "wąkátuya okíchiyusịka," the greatest enemy, was the Khąǧí wichášạ.

My grandmother Turtle Lung Woman told me she sat and thought about her life as she sat and sewed hąpíkceka. She saw life at the "wašícu," at the white man's forts. She knew what "phežúta sápa," meaning "black medicine," coffee, and "aǧúyapi," meaning "burned-on," bread, tasted like. She saw the strange and wonderful things there at the forts. She knew what the white man looked like, but she did not yet dread him. She knew what the Khąǧí wichášạ looked like and she dreaded him the most.

The Khąǧí wichášạ looked like us, only his hair and clothing were different. He wore his hair long, like our men, but the hair on the forehead of the Khąǧí wichášạ was cut into short bangs. He combed it distinctively so that it stood up like a stiff comb on a bird, such as on a ruffed grouse or prairie chicken. His shadow was one that our people had learned to dread. Seeing him so close meant sure death.

The way we thought was not the same as the way the Khąǧí wichášạ thought, even though it seemed we would look the same to any wašícu, or white man, the same to anyone unfamiliar with our culture and theirs. His language and customs were different. The Khąǧí wichášạ wore a necklace of strings of beads cascading down his chest. His beadwork and art were different. The cradle boards we used to carry our babies were similar only in structure, not in decoration. We lived a different way from him.

As far back as anyone remembers, the Khǧí wichášá was always our adversary. He hated us and in time we learned to hate him. The Khǧí wichášá even killed our children and old women who were gathering wood or anyone who was found unprotected. He came lurking into our largest camps. We were on guard always. He would sneak in and claim one of us.

We called it "phe'ícuya zuyá glí" when the men went to war against them, "for a scalp they went to war and came back." "Glípi," we say, "they returned." They would come home and boast that they had killed a Crow. "Eyá héchųs'e, iwóglakapi eš thóka wą wakté iyápi," they would say that they killed a Crow but no one would believe them. So when they killed a Crow they would take a piece of the scalp, put it under their belt, and they would carry it that way. "Thóka phehį yuhá glípi," with the "other people's scalps they came home." The word "thóka" meant "the other people." We used this word to refer, in a general way, to any other tribe other than the Khǧí.

My grandfather Ité Sįyąkhiya made careful preparations before he went with others to war against the Khǧí wichášá. He killed a deer, elk, or buffalo and left the best part of it as a sacrifice to the spirits. He asked the spirits to help him succeed in war. He vowed to take only from the enemy. He wanted to return with more horses and scalps than anyone. If the spirits were pleased they would help him. Otherwise they might help the enemy.

Ité Sįyąkhiya invoked the spirit of "Makhá," the earth. He took white clay from the earth and painted himself for battle. He mixed the white earth with buffalo fat and used it to paint his face and body. While he did this he would sing a song: "Lé makhá wékic'ų kį, ų oyáte iníhąwa yelo." These words mean "This earth I use as paint makes the enemy afraid." When he finished singing his song, he mounted a horse and rode into battle. When he painted himself this way, the dust flying shielded him from enemy eyes.

In his day, every event had a song. It was thought that every Lakota should have a personal song to please the spirits, especially Tákuškąšką, "that which moves, moves" – the energy in all living things, the Lakota God. It was said that Tákuškąšką, like all spirits, loved the voices of men and women in song. He would come and listen and as He listened He would sometimes help those who needed it.

Ité Sįyákhiya sang these songs to remind him of Tákuškąšką. When he sang these songs they reminded him of things infinite in what is finite. It made him aware of the power in the unseen, in Tákuškąšką, that which moves, unseen. In these songs he and the other men would sing about the "šųgmánitu," the wolf, because they thought of themselves as such when they went to war. They lived like a wolf while they roamed the prairie in search of the enemy. They sang these songs to remind themselves that only the earth endured.

So it was Ité Sįyákhiya chose his best horse to take when he went to war. He tied a medicine bundle around its neck. In it he put an herb. He used the root of the "thícanicahu." It is a plant with silver leaves. It grows on the prairie. He fed it to his horse to keep it going on a long journey. For himself, Ité Sįyákhiya brought extra pairs of moccasins and "wasná," pemmican, in a bag made from the stomach of a buffalo. The wasná was made from dried buffalo meat, bone marrow of the buffalo, and dried chokecherries or wild plums. It was pounded together and dried into cakes that are cut and carried. It kept well and nourished him on a long journey into enemy country. He could survive for a while on just water and wasná.

On the day Ité Sįyákhiya went to war, he and the others left quietly at daybreak. They had sent scouts ahead the previous night. They told the scouts where to go, what to do if they saw the enemy, and they told them to return to the main group and tell them everything they saw. Ité Sįyákhiya did not consider it an honor to be asked to join the war party. He felt that the honor would be in coming home victorious.

While they were journeying, Ité Sįyákhiya listened for "wanáǧi," for ghosts. A "wichá wanáǧi" was the spirit of a man who had died. It returned to our world to hover near us, sometimes to warn us of bad things. These things were a mystery to Ité Si̧yák̇hiya. They were "wak̇ȟá," sacred. He knew that his own "naǧí," his spirit, guarded him and warned him of danger. It was this part of him that would one day travel to the spirit world.

It was this, the wanáǧi of his ancestors, those who died, who came back to warn him and the others. If a wanáǧi appeared and sang a victory song, they would be victorious over the enemy. If instead the wanáǧi sang a mourning song, the opposite would be true. Ité Si̧yák̇hiya knew that the wanáǧi traveled at night. He waited with the others until daybreak to leave for war.

When they returned from a successful fight, Ité Si̧yák̇hiya and the other men would stop outside camp and, in full battle array, circle it. Triumphant and proud, they rode on horseback at full speed around the camp. Turtle Lung Woman watched the parade. The horses they rode were often the ones they captured from the enemy. What an honor it was to ride them in front of the women.

Ité Si̧yák̇hiya, like the other men, fought for horses as much as for anything else. He greatly admired the speed and endurance of the "šúkawak̇ḣa," or "sacred dog," the horse. Like all Lakota men, he dreaded Ḣaǧí wicháša horse thieves as much as the Ḣaǧí wicháša dreaded our horse thievery. For this reason, if any Ḣaǧí wicháša were found in our territory, they would be killed immediately.

They participated in a ceremony after they returned from war. It was called the Wakté Aglí Wachípi, the Kills and Returns Dance. In it, the drummers and singers were the warriors returning home victorious from the fight. They carried small drums, the size of small shields. They drummed and sang honoring songs for all the warriors, living and dead.

The dancers were women, lamenting the death of sons or husbands or relatives lost in the fight. They carried on long poles the scalps of the enemy. The theme was vengeance. The men, with their faces painted black, stood with the women in a circle around a tall pole, moving in a direction from right to left.

The women stood side by side, shoulder to shoulder with their scalp sticks, dancing near the men. The men stood together shoulder to shoulder near the women, singing songs of the living and dead heroes. They danced circling the pole in the center. The pole was painted black and white in alternating stripes. The black paint signified that the enemy had been killed. The white stripes indicated victory in battle. The center pole had hanging from it a scalp, a hand, and a foot of the enemy.

I Look For Them

Khǎǧí wicháša kį	The Crow men
owíchawale	I am seeking
iyéwaya	I found them
cha	so
thašų́ke kį	their horses
awákuwe	I bring home

2

Khąǧí Wicháša, Crow Men

Turtle Lung Woman told me a story about the Khąǧí wicháša. She said that there were "Lakhóta oyáte wą wichóthi," that our people made camp in a certain place. It was summer and this particular group decided it was time to seek a better place to camp. There was scarce game in the area and the people were hungry.

There was activity everywhere as everyone made preparations for the move. In those days everything was done a certain way, and it took some time before they actually started out. "Églakapi," they gathered their possessions. They belonged to the woman and it was her responsibility to pack them well. Turtle Lung Woman and the other women visited as they packed everything, including their tipis, tipi poles, and personal things.

It was the woman's work to move everything her family had, all of her belongings. To do this, she constructed a "šúka ú k'ípi," meaning "a dog wears it." This is a pony drag or a travois. She constructed it by bending a sapling into a simple hoop. It measured about four or five feet in length and three to four feet in width. She put webbing on it with rawhide thongs at five-inch intervals to make it strong enough to carry her belongings.

Once she finished it, she attached it to two long tipi poles. She secured it with leather thongs on the poles to form an "A," with the webbed hoop in the center, just under the horse's tail. Her belongings rested on the webbed hoop, which is called "šúka chągléška," meaning that "a horse pulls the wood on which it rests." She attached the top of the "A" to the horse with a harness made of buffalo hide. This harness is attached around the breast of the animal. The thicker portion of the poles at the bottom drag on the ground. In the days before the horse, a dog performed the same task. That is why it is called a "šúka ú k'ípi," meaning "a dog pulled it."

Turtle Lung Woman said she took pride in packing her travois. It required special skill. Once she constructed the base for hers, she packed her belongings on it and tied them on with a leather thong for the move. She took special care in securing it to the horse. She checked the condition of the harnesses before packing it. She said she was constantly aware of the other men and women watching and judging how well she performed her task.

The men decided how the group should proceed once everyone was ready to move. The movement of the camp usually began in the early morning. The "thašíyagnupa," the meadowlark, its distinctive song, awakened everyone at the first light of day. When they finally started out, the procession began with the men on horseback in the lead. The young boys in charge of the herd of horses came behind the men. Then the women and young girls. Last came the young children with the elderly. The horses bearing the travois came with the women. Sometimes young children or the infirm rode on the travois.

Turtle Lung Woman said the journey was always a social event so that everyone could remain in good spirits. They traveled a distance of ten miles or even as far as twenty miles, depending on the condition of the horses. The decision to stop depended on what they set out to accomplish that day. During the day they stopped to rest four times. In everything we did, then and now, the number four had special significance. So it was that the fourth stop was usually the final stop for the day.

They tried to camp near water and firewood. Always, they tried to stay near the buffalo – like the oyáte, the "thatháka" were constantly on the move. They too migrated to better sources of food. The thatháka knew where the best grazing was and they moved if they didn't like where they were. They moved at a slower pace, about two miles in a day, as they grazed on prairie grass, fattening up for the winter and for the great hunts. The great hunts occurred in the autumn. It was then that the people prepared for winter. They had to accumulate enough meat to survive the winter months, when they remained camped in one spot.

We called ourselves Pté Oyáte, or Female Buffalo People. We depended on the buffalo for our way of life. In April when the young buffalo calf was born, the cycle of life on the plains began. In October when the great hunts began, the young calves were mature and we began to accumulate what we needed for the winter. We as a people were aware of these things and lived our lives according to these natural cycles.

Turtle Lung Woman said that when the men were successful in a hunt they came home singing the Buffalo Song. She and the other women joined in. They went to butcher the carcasses after they sang. They were the ones who laid claim to their husband's kill. They skinned the buffalo shot by their husband's or son's arrow. They knew from the way the shaft was decorated whose arrow it was. Once they identified it, the carcass belonged to them. They could do with it as they wished. It provided them with material to make new things or to repair old ones.

It was only the skin of the buffalo that belonged to the woman of the man who killed it. She could also take the brains, tongue, kidney, and liver. The raw kidney and liver were a delicacy for her husband. The brains she used to tan the hide by rubbing it in. The meat of the great animal belonged to all the people. It was common property and everyone had a share in it. The men equally distributed the meat to everyone. The surplus meat was dried for future use as "pápa sáka," dried meat.

The thathąka's hide became our shelter. Indeed, the name "thathąka" means "large hide." We used it to make our tipis. We made our clothing and moccasins from it. We used the fur to make warm robes. We used the thathąka skull for our religious ceremonies. Its horns we made into spoons. Its tongue became a delicacy to eat. We even used its hair for rope. We used every part of the thathąka. Its bones we made into useful tools like hide scrapers and awls. Its sinew we made into bowstrings and thread. We used its stomach as a cooking pot. We even used its dried dung as fuel.

We owed our existence to it. It was a sacred animal given to us by Tákuškąšką. We were its people. We were its spirit embodied. We grew strong from it. We were a handsome people, our men grew tall and strong. Our women were slender-boned and tall, with long legs that kept pace with the children when our camps moved. We women appeared heavy around middle age because of our shorter torso, but our legs were strong and took up the greater part of our bodies. Our children were willowy and tall at the onset of adolescence. It was said that our stamina was enviable, that our bodies had adapted to a hard life on the plains. The buffalo made us strong. We ate every part of it, including the marrow of the bone.

A buffalo hunt was well thought out and was seldom a random event. Our men's sole occupation was to hunt. To hunt this great animal took skill, yet as skilled as they were they never acted alone. The hunt was always communal.

The one thing we had in common with the "hutópa," the "four-legged," the buffalo, was that we, "húnųp," the "two-legged," roamed the land with him, the gently rolling hills and plains, in search of food. They roamed the land in herds, we roamed in "thiyóšpaye," in family groups joined together. There had been great herds in the old days, but they, like us, usually preferred to move in smaller herds. They had common sense and we followed what they did. We learned to be like them because we depended upon them for everything.

This earth we "ikcé oyáte," we common people, call a woman, our mother. It lies in slumber from hunt to hunt, from battle to battle, in the movements of our people from one camp to another. So it seemed the earth slept while we camped in our winter camps, as we chose to remain in one place through the severe winters. In the spring when the grass was red and the buffalo calves were born, the earth came alive again.

The earth we attributed female energy to, both nurturing and mysteriously divine. Her power men dreaded, her love they claimed as theirs. You could put your ear to her breast and hear her sigh. In between the hunt, the battle, and the movement of the camp, she slept. She languished. She lived for the times when our men rode fast on their horses to hunt the buffalo. When they charged on horseback into battle to touch the enemy. When our people walked softly upon her in search of the buffalo. Then the earth came alive. In battle she trembled, in the hunt she arched her spine, in the movement of our camp she danced. These were the times our people were alive the most.

In her story, Turtle Lung Woman told about a Lakota man. He decided to stay when the people moved their camp. "Éna uk'úpi na híhani ki ukíyayikte," he said, "We will stay one more night and in the morning we will follow you." So, he and his wife stayed while the others left.

The day that the man and his wife decided to stay, the people were having a hard time finding buffalo or other game to hunt. They were hungry. The man knew where some buffalo were, so he was thinking he would kill one and take the meat for himself. In his hunger, the man forgot how dangerous it was to camp alone when the Khągí were near. In those days, the Khągí came and preyed on anyone they found alone and unprotected.

The man and his wife stayed in the spot where they had camped when the others left. The man had told the others, "Tókša táku mic'íška," that he had things to do, like repairing his bow and arrows. The word "tókša" meant "by and by" – he would catch up when he could. In a short while, the man busied himself while his wife sat near him.

The man thought about how many arrows he might need to make a swift kill. He tested the strength of his bow made from the wood of an ash tree. His arrows were made from a different kind of wood such as chokecherry, gooseberry, or Juneberry. "Yuzíl wakátakiya yuzí na'iš khútakiya," he would stretch the bow upward as if he were using it to send an arrow flying. He would point it downward and do the same as if he were making his kill from high on a horse.

He thought about how he and his wife would enjoy a feast that night after he killed a buffalo.

He did not see until some time later that someone or something was watching him from his partially closed doorway. He looked again to make sure that it was as he thought. Suddenly something moved outside his tipi and he caught the movement out of the corner of his eye.

A cold feeling came over him as he said to his wife: "Winúȟcala owáži yąká yo," "old woman, sit still." "Winúȟcala," meaning "old woman," was a term used to refer to a wife who had been with a man for a long time. It was an endearing term used by a man to refer to his wife. She in turn called him "wicháȟcala," meaning "old man," in the same way.

"Wichá ištá wą wąbláke," the man said, "I saw a man's eye watching us." The man's worst fear came true. "Do not be alarmed. Act in a normal manner," he warned his wife, "wait for my signal and be ready." He continued working on his bow. Quietly he said, "Tókša," meaning "Wait." As he said this, without betraying his fear, he inserted an arrow into his raised bow, and right where he saw movement he let his arrow fly. "Iyópteya," he aimed it well. A Khąǧí wichášа stood outside the tipi door. They heard him fall. His aim had been good.

The man ran out to see the Khąǧí wichášа's legs jerk as he lay on the ground. The arrow had pierced him in the eye. Soon he was still. The man summoned his wife. When she saw what had happened, the woman grabbed her robes and dried food in a bag. They ran from the tipi. They were always prepared, in those days, for the worst, and their horses stood waiting. He and his wife quickly mounted them.

"Wíyeya égnakapi cha," we say, "They were ready." They took what they needed at a moment's notice, the rest they left behind. They left the tent and fled toward the hills. "Khiglékiya khe," they fled in the direction the main camp had gone.

"Zipáha tháka wą ektá khiyótaka," they found a high hill, where they hid but could still see their abandoned camp. They dismounted their horses. They sat down exhausted. They looked toward the abandoned camp. "Ųkáyapekte lo," he said, "we will spend the night in the open." He did not look forward to it.

After a while they heard loud wailing coming from the abandoned camp. They heard the sound of people mourning the death of the Khąǧí wichášą. They knew the enemy had found the man shot in the eye. They saw smoke and fire coming from the camp. He knew the Khąǧí had set his wife's tipi on fire.

The man and his wife watched their belongings burn. His wife lamented. How long it had taken to sew the buffalo skins for her tipi! She knew they were fortunate to flee with their lives. She knew they would have watched their own people destroy their belongings if they knew what her husband was about to do.

He was going alone to hunt that day. He was going to hunt for himself. It was against everything his people believed. The consequence for acting alone would have been the destruction of their property. Perhaps he would have lost his life as well. He thought of those things as he watched his belongings burn.

After a while he and his wife mounted their horses and left. "Héchel glápi," they started after their people. The followed the trail the others left. They were determined to catch up to them before the mourning Khąǧí caught up to them.

The man knew he was no match against two or more angry Khąǧí wichášą. They would be seeking reprisal. He traveled swiftly toward the main camp. There was one thing the man took when he fled. "Phehį yuhá khe" – he had the enemy's scalp.

When they reached the main camp he rode in displaying the phehį. "Ektá khihųni khe," he rejoined them, and he told them everything that had happened to them. He warned them that the Khąǧí wichášą may be on their way to where they were. He told them to make preparations for an attack. He said the Khąǧí were looking for retribution.

A Stone Nation Is Speaking

Tuwá	Someone
tókhiya tákeya lo	somewhere is speaking
wazíyataŋ	from the north
thuŋká oyáte waŋ	a sacred-stone nation
i'á	is speaking
nayáȟ'uŋpikte	you will hear
tuwá	someone
tókhiya	somewhere
tákeya lo	speaking

3

Turtle Lung Woman

When my grandmother Turtle Lung Woman was small the people believed in extraordinary things. The medicine men and women were able to make miraculous things happen. As with all Lakota "wakháyeža," or "sacred beings," which is the name for children, she grew up believing in the mystical, in the magical stories of how things came to be.

Turtle Lung Woman said she had a dream about an "íyą," or "sacred stone." In the dream the íyą asked her to make a pouch for it and to line the pouch with a special herb. In this pouch the íyą would dwell. It asked her to carry the pouch in a medicine bag that she must make to keep healing herbs and roots in.

Turtle Lung Woman, as dreamer, listened well. She knew the power of íyą. Íyą lived in the realm of spirit, of the unseen and the unknown. She knew that it meant no harm. It came to her for a reason. She wanted to honor it. She wanted to be its hands, feet, and eyes. It said that her eyes would see beyond the realm of her natural vision. She would be able to seek and find things, even people who had disappeared mysteriously. It told her that her feet would travel far into the future without ever leaving her home. She would be able to predict future events. It said her hands would heal. She would be given a "waphíye," a healing gift, to help others.

Turtle Lung Woman, as dreamer, said she responded to the íyą before awakening. She heard herself say to the íyą that she would do as it asked. She heard herself, but she did not fully know what this would mean for her. She did not know how to articulate her dream once she awakened. She said nothing about the dream at first to anyone. The íyą came to her. She made a pouch for it. She used its power. In time, its helpers came and she used them too. The people said about her, "Íyą eyá yuhá," meaning, "She had some sacred stones that she uses when she needs help."

My grandmother Turtle Lung Woman was born on the plains, on the land that stretched from one corner of the earth to the other. In this vastness, she saw how the old myths, which told of how the four winds traveled along the rim of the earth to establish their directions, could have been. She could see the edge of the earth, along the horizon where it stretched around the earth like a tight band. It held the sky to the earth. Where the two met, a visible path appeared along the rim of the earth. It was most visible at dawn and again at dusk.

She grew up believing that it was along this route that the four brothers who established the four sacred directions traveled. She knew how the directions came to be. She knew how everything found its name and place on this earth. She knew it was all as it should be, nothing was random. It had to be so. It was the way the Lakotas thought. There was order in all things. There was cause and effect. There was meaning in all things. She knew that all things could tell their own stories. Their own legends about how they came to be.

It was in those days that my grandmother Turtle Lung Woman was a child. She sat playing with her dolls, small tipi, and small buffalo bladder pots. She carried the things women carried. For a small girl these things were miniature versions of what the women had. They were in usable shape, and as she played with them, she was practicing skills she would need in her later life as a woman. She even had a miniature work bag in which she kept tools to make moccasins for her dolls. In time, she acquired the skills necessary to make real moccasins.

Turtle Lung Woman, as a young girl, had long hair that she wore a certain way. Her hair was straight and black. It was parted down the center and on each side her mother carefully braided it in two long braids. These were often plastered to her back as she ran here and there in play.

She wore a buckskin dress tailored by her mother to grow with her. The awl-punched holes in the buckskin had two small sets of holes so that as she grew larger, the seams could be adjusted to fit her. The hem of the dress looked uneven, with the longer fringes on both sides and the shorter ones in the center. It allowed freedom of movement. She could run in the dress. As a young girl she played freely.

Turtle Lung Woman, as a girl, played under the watchful eyes of her "ųcí," her grandmother. It was Ųcí who reminded her of the proper behavior if she deviated from it. If her mother was busy with chores and other responsibilities, she stayed near her ųcí. More often than not, she was with her friends.

She had her group of girl friends who played together. They stayed in small groups and took short walks around the camp or went swimming together in the summer. They played and imitated the women, doing everything they did. They gave mock feasts and tended to dolls carried in cradle boards, singing songs to them and braiding their hair in neat braids. They played games together, enjoying each other's company. They did not play with the boys. "Él éwichawatųwąpišni," she said, "We ignored them." The boys disregarded them in turn. They were in their own world as well. Theirs was a male world, filled with play on horses and games of aggression. They too roamed in small groups. They learned early how to care for and ride horses.

In many ways their lives were like those of the girls. They played freely, imitating the adults around them, especially their fathers, uncles, and older brothers in order to master life-long skills. A boy learned early to hunt. He learned how to find and kill small game. It was a skill he would need, just like knowing how to skin the hide of a buffalo was an important skill for a girl. Although a boy disregarded the girls, as he grew older, he, like most adolescent boys, dreamed of "wi'óyuspe," how to capture a young girl in courtship. In time, he would even be willing to give away his prized horse for a girl he loved.

My grandmother Turtle Lung Woman knew that if she told me about these things, I would remember. If she told me about her childhood, I would listen. If she told me about how the people lived back then, I would remember. If she mentioned in passing a story about the way things were done when she was small, I would not forget. I would laugh with her at a funny story she told. She was my ųcí. She saw herself in me. I saw how she cared about me. "Thakóža," she called me, "grandchild." It was an honored name.

When I knew Turtle Lung Woman, she seemed to me to embody everything she told me about the old ways. She herself was the old way, fast disappearing. She spoke the only language she knew. Her Lakota words reflected a different worldview. She knew what life meant by defining it that way. The essence of everything we were, our way of life, was embedded in the old words she spoke.

"Thawóglake hená slolwáye," I remember her words well. The things she told me. In time I knew all the things she spoke of in that old way. I knew her stories well. "Eháni wóglake," she spoke of a time long past. "Eháni wichó'ų kį awóglake," she spoke of how, in the old way, the people conducted themselves.

Her Lakota name was Kheglézela Chağúwį: "Kheglézela," meaning "spotted turtle that lives on land," "Chağú," meaning "lung," and "Wį," meaning "woman." In the tribal rolls her name is Turpine Light because someone read her name wrong. How one reads "Turpine Light" instead of "Turtle Lung," I will never know.

Turtle Lung Woman always kept her name. "Chažé gluhá," she carried her name like she carried the old way. "Eháni oyáte kį héchel wichó'ų. Nakų hignáthųpi eš eyá chažé gluhápi," a long time ago, that was the way the people lived. So that even if she was married, the woman kept her name, as Turtle Lung Woman did to her death.

She was a small woman. "Ptécelala," we say, "short in stature." "Héhą wąbláke," I saw her when I was growing up. I observed her and how she lived. I remember the way she wore long dresses, with sleeves down to her wrists and a high collar so that nothing showed up to her chin. The hem of her dress came down over cloth leggings and canvas moccasins.

Turtle Lung Woman owned three pairs of moccasins. She had one pair for ordinary use. A second pair for special outings. She had a third pair for traditional dancing. Her moccasins that she had for ordinary wear were made of canvas, when I knew her. By then, we no longer hunted buffalo, and the women made moccasins with the strongest material on hand. Her canvas moccasins had leather trimmings. The heel and toe of the moccasins were leather. The other two pair of moccasins she had were leather. These were made in the old way. They were beaded in bold geometric designs. She also wore stockings with her moccasins. She wore over them red or blue felt leggings that matched her moccasins.

She braided her long dark hair in two neat braids. The way she wore her hair when she was a young girl. Her hair was not white but still had color in it when I knew her. I watched the way she combed it. How careful she was not to drop one hair on the ground. She did not want anyone taking it and using it against her. She thought that someone with ill will might take a part of her and wish evil on her. She believed, as all Lakotas believed, that a person's hair contained the essence of that person and should be treated with respect. So, she took all the hair that fell from the comb and carefully gathered it and threw it into the fire.

She wore an old Lakota belt, the kind that belonged to Lakota women like her. In the old days, she told me, she hung a "míla ožúha," a knife sheath, on her belt. She also had a "thahį́špa," an awl case with an awl in it, and a "wípağuka," a scraper for scraping hide. She had a tool to "ka'íle," or "make a fire," that she carried. These were her tools, she said, the things she needed in her household.

Turtle Lung Woman was a traditional dancer. She traveled to many dances, "wachí ománi." The word "wachí," means "to dance." The word "ománi" means "to travel." She wore a buckskin dress when she danced in the traditional way. It was tanned almost white so that it was beautiful, pleasing to the eye. "Owáyag wašté," we say, "good to see." She also wore beaded leather leggings that we called "hųská," meaning "long in length," referring to the fringes in the leggings. She wore leather moccasins with geometric designs beaded on them.

She carried a shawl with long fringes. Her shawl and the way she danced reminded me of an old song: "Į́kpata nawáž̇į na šína chícoze, má'eya, má'eya, léchi kú wa na." The words mean, "I stand at the end and swing my shawl for you, listen to me, hear me, come home this way." The fringes on her shawl swayed rhythmically as she danced slowly and deliberately. "Má'eya, má'eya, léchi kú wa na."

Owl

Hįhą	Owls
hothų pelo	hooting
hąhépi hiyáye cį	in the passing of the night
hįhą	owls
hothų pelo	hooting

4

Stones and Turtle Shells

A dream came to her. It came at night, like an owl. It was a clear dream. She saw it the way an owl sees at night. She gained power from it. The power she gained was not that of a man. Hers was a gentle strength. The way an owl flies at night, its soft feathers moving without sound. She saw wisdom in her dream. She vowed to be like that. She would imitate the ways of the owl. She would treat those who came to her for help that way. The way an owl's soft feathers move over the night wind, her hands would move over the spirit of the person who came to her for help. It was the "naǧí," the spirit, that she healed. It was always this that required healing. She knew if her healing did not work, "hihá hothúpi, hahépi hiyáye ci hihá hothúpi," the owls would hoot in the passing of the night, then call out. If the owl hoots twice – someone will die.

In her dream she was told how to do certain things. "Lakhol waphíye," how to heal the old way. In the dream, an íya came to her and told her what to do. Íya is a friend of Tákuškaška, "that which is, moves," the Creator. Since the íya is "kholá," a friend, to Tákuškaška, it knows everything and it can find anyone or anything that is lost. Turtle Lung Woman listened to the íya in her dream. She did as she was told. The íya who spoke to her said it was a spirit that came from "thuká," a stone that fell from the sky.

The way people count their age in Lakota is by the number of "waníyetu," or "winters," survived. The winters in the 1920s and 1930s were severe. The blizzards blew through the prairie in unpredictable ways. When the snows fell no one went too far from their homes.

Turtle Lung Woman wrapped a blanket around herself during those winters. "Khilíya osní," we say, "it is incredibly cold." The blanket she wrapped around herself was like a coat. She did it to keep warm. It was not an ordinary blanket but a beautiful one. "Líla ehą́ni," a long time ago, she would have wrapped a buffalo robe around herself, using the fur side in. The skin side of the buffalo painted with geometric designs in bold patterns of red, yellow, black, blue, and green. These she painted herself, having lived through many winters. She was "nacá," or "wise."

The way she stood holding the blanket around herself reminded me of how I saw them bind her in a blanket and lower her to the floor of her small cabin. The way it is done in a Yuwípi ceremony. She did the Yuwípi ceremony. She conducted it. The íyą she had enabled her to practice this ritual to call forth the sacred stones and use them to help others.

Turtle Lung Woman prepared for the Yuwípi ceremony as any medicine person would. "Pheẑúta wį́yą hécha," she was a medicine woman herself. The word "pheẑúta" means "medicine." She knew the old medicine. "Wóphiye yuhá," she was a healer, a conduit, a channel for conveying good. She was not an ordinary person. This knowledge came to her in dreams. She fulfilled their requirements and practiced these ways. Her curing occurred in ways that one would not notice immediately. They happened when the person being healed realized that she had rid them of the negative energy inherent in their ailment. In that way, her job of healing was easy, everything was either "waẑté niẑ waẑtéẑni," good or not so, beneficial or harmful, light or darkness. Once she helped the patient perceive one or the other, healing could occur. "Táku cha olé héchi iyéyįkte," whatever the patient inherently sought, they would find.

There were certain things she kept in a special bag. It was her "wóphiye," her medicine bag, and it was considered sacred. It was said that wóphiye is a sacred place where only good dwells and nothing evil lives there. It was what she had, a wóphiye to take where she needed. So that wherever she went she brought only good with her when she brought her wóphiye.

34

In her wóphiye she had, among other things, the íyą, the sacred stones that came into her possession. They were her helpers. "Há yuhá," she also had turtle shells. She used them in her ceremonies. To her these were not just mere turtle shells. They embodied the spirit of the animal. They were her helpers as well.

The name Spotted Turtle Lung Woman referred to the spotted turtles that walked on land. Indeed they were the ancient turtles that roamed the plains in earlier times. They had always existed there on the flat arid land. In a certain part of Nebraska, you can still find them roaming the land, as they have done from a time long past.

She believed, as all Lakotas did, that death existed only on this plane, that on another level, spirit existed forever. So, certain things were true in our Lakota world, like a feather from an eagle retains the original spirit of the bird, the same with a hair from a horse's tail. Even one single strand retained the whole spirit of the animal, the spirit that existed forever.

We call the horse "šųkawakhą," or "sacred dog." Its hair was sometimes used to decorate clothing. It symbolized bravery. The eagle feather, especially the tail feathers of the golden eagle, when worn by a warrior, signified great courage. Turtle Lung Woman believed this about the turtle shells. They were sacred to her, just as the eagle feather, hair from a horse's tail, or any other thing taken from a bird or animal, is sacred to a medicine man or woman using it. The way she believed her own hair was sacred and she disposed of it properly. She did not want anyone who felt ill will toward her to find a strand of her hair and use it against her. It was the same with the turtle shells that she used as spirit helpers in her ceremonies. They helped her in many ways.

When the ceremony began, she was bound and laid at the altar where the íyą and the turtle shells were kept. "Lená táku yuhá kį, ékignaka, yusnípi chą wįkcekce áta ománipi škhe," when the light in the room was extinguished it was said that the things she placed at the altar moved in mysterious ways. The people in the ceremony could hear them walking in the room, the way they moved on land, slowly and deliberately they walked. Their steps moved rhythmically to the sound of the earth breathing. An ancient breath that one could see in the mist in the early morning. So the spotted turtles moved, they danced to the sound of life, in the ceremony they were heard by everyone present.

When this happened the person for whom the ceremony was held could expect miracles. He whom she had summoned came, and she welcomed Him. She knew no fear, for He did not come that way but appeared when one prayed in a quiet and persistent way, the way Turtle Lung Woman breathed life into the empty shells. She breathed on them gently, and they came alive for her. She invoked their spirit and they came to her aid. In the Yuwípi ceremony, her helpers that only she could see came and set her free from the blanket she was wrapped in. When there was light in the room again, everyone saw that she was no longer bound. The íyą and empty turtle shells sat at the altar, where they had been when the ceremony began. It was as if nothing happened, indeed nothing that ordinary eyes could see. What the eyes did not see could still be perceived by the heart and was as real as the sound of the ancient turtles walking on sandy shores in a faraway time and place. The place where Turtle Lung Woman must have gone to find a cure.

My grandmother Turtle Lung Woman's wóphiye was made potent by the proper ceremony. Hers was a deerskin bag decorated with lazy stitch beadwork in red, blue, black, green, and yellow. The design was simple, alternating colors with white beads. It looked plain. White beads trimmed the opening and a leather thong was used to secure the top. She kept her medicine in it, wrapped in small leather pouches and tied securely. She also had in her medicine bag a small bone spoon to use in giving the medicine to the sick. The spoon and pouches were small, and she kept other things in her medicine bag. In it she kept the íyą and the turtle shells. She had a sacred pipe, a medicine rattle, and a small drum. She also had "wasná," pemmican, for spirit food. It was the same pemmican the men took with them when they went to war.

"Wasná" means "pounded." This refers to the way in which it was made. It was made with dried buffalo meat and chokecherries or wild plums pounded together. She carried a staff of cherry wood in her medicine bag to help her find chokecherries and wild plums to make the wasná. The pemmican was sweet from the chokecherry or plum juice, and sometimes we children begged her for some. It was a real treat to take a handful of the wasná and suck the sweetness out of it like hard candy. She would sometimes indulge us and let us have some.

We, her family, helped her by watching her sacred things carefully. "Otúyacį gnákapišni," these things were not kept for ordinary purposes. They had to be treated with respect. They had to be treated like the sacred objects that they were. If a young woman was present who was in the midst of her menses, Turtle Lung Woman would put the medicine bag away. She seemed to know. "Thạkál ékhignake," she would even go as far as to remove it from the room. She would set it outdoors where nothing could influence its power.

The things she carried in it were required for someone who worked with the old medicine. When women came to her for help, she would listen carefully to their problems. A long time ago, there were few diseases, and Turtle Lung Woman specialized in problems women faced. From the way the woman spoke, if Turtle Lung Woman listened carefully and long enough, she would gain enough information to procure a cure. "Hạ," she would say, at the right moment and with the right meaning. That one word, "Hạ," could mean, "Yes, I see," or "I understand," or "So it is." That one simple statement, "Hạ," meant she was giving all of her attention to every detail the patient was telling. If she listened carefully and long enough, the truth would reveal itself. To Turtle Lung Woman disease was not a random occurrence but something that had a cause, that somewhere at some time a decision was made that led to the present condition. If she examined when and why that was so, she would be able to pinpoint a cure. Indeed, she seemed to know the disease and its remedy. She knew what to do.

I once watched her. She looked at the woman for a while before she did anything. The way an owl's eyes can look only forward. She did not move her eyes from the woman for a long while, as if she could see through her. She then took her sacred pipe and prayed with it to the four directions. She took smoke from it and blew it into the turtle shell. She knew that the smoke was pleasing to all living things and that the spirit of the turtle would look with favor on everything she was doing. This was her "waphíya," meaning "her way to heal." Indeed the words taken literally can mean "to repair."

She tried to heal using her turtles and her waphíya. Sometimes she used her "phežúta," the herbs she used, her medicine. She carried many kinds of roots, things that looked like dried roots of plants that I could not name. She found these on the prairie. She prepared the medicine root to be administered. She would sing a song while she was doing this. The woman remained in the room with her. She sang a song, reassuring the woman who came to her, telling her that the medicine would heal her. She sang like the man who saw the "mathó," the bear, digging for roots in the Ȟé Sápa, the Black Hills. The bear seeks and finds for us many of the medicines we use to heal our sick.

She gave the patient the roots and herbs she prepared. She sang all the while. Her voice low and calming. She did not sing the tremolo, the way only Lakota women know how to do. The way an owl's voice can be. How an owl calls at night with a tremulous voice. It hoots as it feeds on live prey. No, she did not sing the tremolo. She knew that some diseases were stronger by night and others by day, like the owl and the spotted turtle that walks on land. In her dreams she saw them both.

She sang softly at times, a sigh. Her voice growing stronger as she reassured the woman that the medicine she gave would heal. She took the "wagmúha," the medicine rattle made from a turtle's shell, and shook it gently. The way I have heard it in some ceremonies. It is used to keep away the bad spirit causing the illness. Whatever caused the woman to be ill hears the sacred sound of the rattle and it flees. The same way, they say, a bad spirit would not like the sound of the "cháčheǧa," the drum, and the "šíyothąka," the flute.

When she finished giving the woman the medicine she prepared, she sang a final song. A song that tells the woman the illness is conquered. Softly she prayed, "Wóyazą hená hiyáb iyáyįkte," "the pain will go away from you." I have heard that when she did this, even fevers sometimes disappeared. Turtle Lung Woman in her ceremonies tended primarily to women. "Tókhi wíyą waží thamáhel héchel šíca hátą aphíya cha," so if a woman came to her with internal problems, she would perform this healing ceremony. "Wóphiya wį́yą hécha," for she was truly a medicine woman.

"Ho, hé slolwáye," that was what I knew of her. Like all medicine men and women she received some compensation for what she did. It was how she lived. It was said that all medicine men and women were expected to live an honorable life, to be of good character. They had to be unblemished, the way the snow falls on the plains, untouched. It lays upon the earth, cleansing it of impurities. It heals. That's why when it doesn't snow during a dry spell in the winter people get sick. The snow, cold and pure, comes and cleanses the earth.

The same way, a medicine man or woman can cleanse one of impurities of mind or body and procure a healing. They can do this only if they do it the right way. If they, themselves, are pure of heart. If they lived this way, they would live good, long lives, it was said. If they didn't they would not see old age. Turtle Lung Woman saw old age. "Wį́yą wakhą́ hécha," she was indeed a sacred woman.

The Song of the Owl and Crow

Hạyétu	At night
mawáni nụwé	may I roam
thatóheya	against the winds
mawáni nụwé	may I roam
hạyétu mawáni	at night I roam
hịhą́	an owl
hothų́hạ	hoots
mawáni nụwé	may I roam
Ą́pa'o	At dawn
mawáni nụwé	may I roam
thatóheya	against the winds
mawáni nụwé	may I roam
ą́pa'o	at dawn
mawáni	I roam
khạǧí	a crow
hothų́hạ	calls
mawáni nụwé	may I roam

5

Wakíyela, The Mourning Dove

Turtle Lung Woman had certain animals she kept, including some turtles, a small bird, a few dogs, and many horses. She kept some of these animals for her enjoyment and companionship. The horses and dogs she kept for practical purposes. They were useful in her household. She kept the turtles for reasons only she knew.

The word for turtle is "kheglézela," and it means "spotted turtle that walks on land." It was said that the turtles she had did her bidding. She was able to make them walk. It was thought that they did her bidding even after they died. We Lakotas believed that its naǧí returns to the spirit world, where the Creator dwells, if it is a good animal like the turtle, bird, dog, or horse. If it is a bad animal, like a wolf or snake, its naǧí does not go there. The spirit of the kheglézela returns to the Creator, but it comes back to help us. Turtle Lung Woman knew that and she relied on her turtles to help her.

When I was a child, I saw how she was with her animals. I saw them as her friends, especially the kheglézela. The way she held them in her hands. They responded to her instantly. She knew them well. She told me the kheglézela are wise, they listen but do not tell secrets. This wisdom Turtle Lung Woman seemed to have. She said the kheglézela's "há," the shell, is thick and nothing can pierce it. She seemed to be telling me to be thick-skinned, like the kheglézela, to get by in life.

Turtle Lung Woman was a medicine woman. She learned from the spirits, they spoke to her in a familiar way. She sought knowledge from dreams, how to use the powers that came from them. She knew the mysterious, how to summon help so that she could use things, and sometimes people, to do her bidding.

It was thought that she could cure, and sometimes others who thought less of her thought that she could make her enemies sick. She knew the roots of the earth and the plants that had their home in the earth. She knew the blossoms of the flowers that were medicinal. It was said that the spirit of the earth was good to her.

When she called to them, the kheglézela came to her aid. They were her spirit helpers. The way she summoned them into her ceremonies. The way people say they hear them walking in the dark. How mysterious is the sound of the kheglézela moving in the dark! When a turtle died, she used every part of it. She kept its shell to use in her ceremonies. She would set it down and breathe into it in a certain way. She dried its heart and ground it into a powder. She used it on cuts or open wounds. She dried it, pounded it, and put it into a drink for healing. She was a capable woman and others came to her for help. If you came to her and did as she said, she could do things for you.

The dogs and horses she kept for practical purposes. The dogs we call "šúka" and the horses "šúkawakhą," or "holy dogs." In the old days the dogs did the work that horses later did for us. They transported the things we packed on travois, all our personal belongings and even our tipis. When the horses took over the work of the dogs, we relied on the horses for much more. They became a part of us, like an arm or leg, and it was hard to think that we could ever live without them. So it was, they were sacred or holy to us, like the turtle. Their spirits sometimes came to us in ceremonies and spoke to us.

Turtle Lung Woman was emotionally attached to her dogs. She liked their disposition, for they are by nature a kind and forgiving animal. They see through our thoughtless cruelty by responding always to our true nature. How alike we are, the dog and humanity. We share that same longing to forgive, in order to survive. "Akícikthųža ye," we say, in the feminine voice, "Forgive him his errors." In all things Lakota, there exists the feminine and the masculine; so too in our language. Where a man would say, "Yo," in asking for forgiveness, meaning, "Do it!" a woman implores, "Ye," in the female voice, "Would you?"

The dog lives that way, possessing the ability to forgive and forget. My grandmother Turtle Lung Woman told me that was why it was a sacred animal in some of our ceremonies. So it was, its spirit came into our ceremonies and spoke to us.

As she grew older, she preferred the company of her animals. Her dogs followed her everywhere she went. It was not unusual to see several of them with her as she walked around her home, tending her household, horses, and land. Even now when I look toward the creek where she lived, I still expect to see her walking toward her house from the creek. "Mayá aglágla thí," her house was near the ravine. She walked down there for water for her horses and dogs. I remember once my father told her a couple of the dogs she had might have the mange. It didn't bother her. They were her friends, regardless. She was like that. She looked beyond the obvious to enjoy what no one else was able to see. For that reason she enjoyed her animals more than anyone I knew. In turn, they trusted her and seemed to do her bidding in surprising ways.

The small bird she had was from the pigeon family, a mourning dove. The Lakota word for a mourning dove is "wakíyela." "Kiyéla" means "it flies." She kept it for a pet, that small wild dove with a mournful call and soft feathers. She named it Wakíyela. It had a stout body, small head, and short legs. It was a peculiar bird, like everything she had, it seemed more special because it was hers.

There were many different kinds of birds that lived near us, some more special than others. The Lakota word for bird is "zitkála." In the old days we wore feathers in our hair to signify that we are relatives to the birds. In our stories we were told that in the beginning of time there was a great race to see who would preside over nature, and we human beings were paired with the zitkála against the buffalo. The race was held, it was said, at the heart of the earth, the center of our universe, the Ȟé Sápa, the Black Hills. It is said that the great circle is still there. In that race the human beings and ziṭkála won. Since then, we have been as relatives.

There were those like the "waḃlígleška," the spotted eagle, that all had talons, they were alike. The birds with talons knew how to get their prey, and our men imitated them when they went on the hunt or to war. There were those like the "šiyáka," teal duck, and the other types of birds that swam in water, they flocked together. There were those like the "šiyó," the prairie grouse, that rested on the ground and were alike. And finally those that nested above the ground like the "pšipšícala ikpíska," the split-tail swallow, which before a storm hovers over us, flocked together. All of them had their own way of life and their own calls or songs. They were like us. We, too, congregated together often. It was the way we survived. We were like the birds, we had our own songs and lived a certain way. A long time ago we were as numerous as they. It is not so, today.

It was said that "líla eháni," in the old days, in a time long past, when the world first began, there was only Tákuškaška, that which moves, and Wí, the Sun, Makhá, the Earth, and Íya, the Rock. It was then that there were no directions on the world as we know them now, so that Wí went down where it pleased. The sun did not rise in the east or set in the west because those directions had not been established. So it rose where it wanted. The light that heralded its coming, what we call "kabléza ácha," dawn, announced its rising wherever it appeared, and at night twilight appeared wherever it set. There was no set direction that one could expect it to appear or disappear.

It was said that day existed then as did night to mark the two divisions of time. "Haẃí," moon, or as we call it, "night sun," indicated time for us, too. The moon, as it traveled to a point farthest from the sun to when it was closest to the sun, marked time for us by its waxing and waning. We kept track of time from full moon to new moon and marked that time as one moon. But the moon, like the sun, used to appear where it wanted in the sky because there were no directions. It was random and chaotic.

It was then that Tákuškąšką decided that something should be done about this. He asked Thaté, Wind, to send his four sons, who were quadruplets, to establish the four directions as we know them today: west, north, east, and south. The four brothers lived with their father. Thaté loved his sons, the eldest being Wazíyata, North; then Wiyóhiyąpa, East; Itókaǧa, South; and then came Wiyóȟpeyata, West. The brothers were told to travel along the edge of the world to establish the four sacred directions in the order of their birth.

They were to divide into four quarters the never-ending circle as seen in the lit dome over "makhá," the earth. The four quarters were to be an equal distance from one another. Once this was done, they were each to select a quarter to preside over. So that, although he was not the firstborn, Wiyóȟpeyata established the first direction where the sun sets each day. Then came Wazíyata, who presides over the north. It was said that Wazíyata, because he was by nature a cruel person, lost his birthright. He would have been the first in all things and to have first choice in everything. Wiyóhiyąpa presides over the direction where the sun rises each day, and Itókaǧa was given the direction where the sun stood at midday, which is the direction from where all pleasant things come. There they dwell forever, the four brothers who were messengers for Tákuškąšką. It is said that they can travel anywhere to all things.

When the four brothers accepted their task, from the time they left their father's house to when they completed their assignment, one year had passed. It took each brother approximately three moons to establish a direction. Thus, not only did they fix a direction to preside over, they also established the year as a division of time. The year according to our time is thirteen moons, beginning in the first moon of spring, which lasts two moons, then comes summer, which lasts four moons, then comes autumn, which lasts two moons, then comes winter, which lasts five moons. Before the brothers established the four directions, we had only day, night, and one moon or month to mark time for us.

It was said that the four brothers were each given a portion of the year to govern. So that Wazíyata, North, presides over the winter months. His cruel wind kills many things, including, it is said, the infant clouds that are born and their infant spirits that are seen in the north, the aurora borealis, the northern lights. The direction Wazíyata presides over represents a hard life. Itókaǧa, South, governs the summer, when the warm southern winds bring the birds home to the north. His direction represents a good life. It is never necessary to invoke his help, he is by nature helpful. Wiyóȟpeyata lives in the west, and with him dwell Wakíya, the thunder beings. They live on the same high mountain and they travel together. Wiyóhiyapa, East, knows all things, it is said, because the sun and moon see all things and relay all they know to him. His is the direction one faces to ask for good health.

When the four brothers were each given a direction to preside over, íya, stones, were placed in each direction: west, north, east and south. Upon these stones a bird landed, and it became the messenger for that direction. In the west, a "pšipšícala ikpíska," a swallow, landed on Wiyóȟpeyata's pile of stones. It is the bird that hovers over us before a storm. In the north, an "ukcékhiha," or "magpie," landed on Wazíyata's pile of stones. It is the bird that is thought to be a bad omen. To the east, a "hihá," an owl, landed on Wiyóhiyapa's pile of stones. It is the bird that sees in the darkness and flies silently to catch its prey. Finally, to the south, a "thašíyagnupa," or "meadowlark," landed on Itókaǧa's pile of stones. It is the bird that sings like the music of Itókaǧa's flute, which he plays when he is in love. These birds, the swallow, magpie, owl, and meadowlark, became the messengers for the four brothers, the four sacred winds.

In our tribe, birds have always been mysterious to us and therefore "wakhá," sacred. Sometimes it was thought that in dreams birds could speak the language of the sacred. It was also thought that men could change themselves into birds, like the bird we call "škípipi," the chickadee. The way a chickadee flew to the poles of the tipi, in the old days. How it perched there and peered into the tipi, as if it were a messenger for a mysterious being.

It was considered a bad omen if a bird flew into someone's tipi or house. Some said if it did this, it was better to take its life. It was thought that something terrible would happen to someone in the household where it flew in. Turtle Lung Woman told me of an old woman who took a bird that flew into her tipi. She killed it and rubbed its blood over the entrance. The old woman thought that if she did this it would prevent evil spirits from entering. Turtle Lung Woman could not bear the thought of her Wakíyela meeting the same fate. Her bird was not that way. It was not a wild bird that flew into her house. She invited it into her house, into her life.

They were together often. I don't know why but she was close to that bird. They lived together like that. She seemed to take for granted things that we noticed about Wakíyela that seemed odd, things that birds didn't normally do but that her bird did and she accepted as normal. I wanted to ask her why she chose the bird to be her companion, but like all Lakota children, I could only observe and wonder, patiently waiting for the opportunity to see the answer for myself.

When Turtle Lung Woman lived alone, her one constant companion at home was Wakíyela, her bird. When she walked anywhere, Wakíyela would fly in front of her for a distance and land on something. There it would sit and wait for her. When she returned again, the bird would know and would fly in front of her. It would land near her again. It seemed to be welcoming her home. It seemed glad to see her return.

One day, while we were gone, something happened to Wakíyela. It was in the summer. Turtle Lung Woman was home with her bird and the other animals. We left to find work in the farm fields in Nebraska. We packed a large canvas tent, tent poles, and other necessities on my father's wagon and left the reservation for many months. We traveled with my aunts and uncles and their families.

We traveled to a place called Tháȟca Wakpá, or Deer Creek. It was a day's ride by wagon. Halfway there, we crossed the state line into Nebraska. We camped at Deer Creek first, and from there we found work in the nearby fields. We worked all summer and autumn for farmers who paid us in cash or crops. We bought mostly food with the money we made. If a farmer gave us sacks of potatoes in pay, we took it back to the reservation and stored it for the long winter.

We were like the birds who flew before Wazíyata, the cold north wind. They migrated south, knowing where to go to find warmer weather and food. We left the isolation of the reservation where they put us. We too traveled in the direction of Itókaǧa, the south wind. We had forgotten what the people had said long ago, how the birds used to fly to Itókaǧa, who presided over the pleasant winds. How they would beg him for help when Wazíyata, whose touch kills everything, pursues them. By then we no longer called to the sacred directions for help like we used to.

When our family traveled during the summer, Turtle Lung Woman stayed home on the reservation, watching the horses and keeping watch over my father's house. In those days there were no thieves so my father did not fear them. I think Turtle Lung Woman didn't want to travel from work camp to work camp with us. So she stayed home. She had no one to depend on, except Wakíyela, her bird.

My father would check on her when he came back to add food to what we were saving for the winter. When my father earned enough money to buy food in large quantities, he would ride back to the reservation to store it. In those days we had what we called "root cellars" where food, especially things like potatoes and squash, was kept since we had no refrigerators. In those days, men like my father were always thinking of ways to have enough food to survive the long winter. Our culture determined a person's age by the numbers of winters survived because the winters were severe. Wazíyata, the North Wind, made sure of that.

One day, while alone during one of the times that my father was away, Turtle Lung Woman was fixing her bed for the night. "Phikhíyahị na," she spread her robes and blankets on her bed and went to lie down. She saw something in her quilts. She watched it move, "o'ípazigzig higláhạ cha," it moved the blanket as it hopped up and down. She said to herself, "Tóškhe lé ịš táku wạ lé táku ȟ'ạ," "What is this thing doing?"

She thought it was a mouse that had come in from the cold night. "Áta okát'a khe," she took her hand and swatted it as it moved under her covers. It immediately stopped moving and Turtle Lung Woman pulled the covers back satisfied that she had stunned the mouse and was preparing to put it out the door. "Yuǧá icú yúkhą Wakíyela he," she looked under the blanket and saw it was Wakíyela, her bird. "Thahú wéǧa ú ȟpá khe," it lay with its neck broken. When she saw what had happened, she reached out and took the small bird in her hands. She cradled its still-warm body in her cold hands. "Gluháha yąkį na chéyahą khe. Iyé cha kat'é," she sat with it and cried for a long time. She could not undo what she did.

Song of a Ghost

Hé naké	Regretfully
wachéye	I weep
hé naké	regretfully
wachéye	I weep
hé naké	regretfully
wachéye	I weep
chéya omáwani	weeping I roam
khoškálaka	among young men
wi'óyuspapi chạ	when they capture young women
iyótạ wacámi k'ụ	I thought myself the best
iyótạ wacámi k'ụ	I thought myself the best
chéya omáwani	weeping I roam

6

Ité Sįyákhiya's Wives

My grandfather Ité Sįyákhiya, Paints His Face with Clay, had many wives. A tall, handsome man, he took pride in fathering many children. He was like other Lakota men who took pride in certain things. They measured their worth in how many horses they stole, how many wives they had, and, always, in killing the enemy. My grandfather's worth was established by his own prowess in obtaining the things he valued. His currency was the horse. A horse could "buy" him a wife. A swift horse helped him in times of war. He liked a fast horse. Perhaps to run from the wives he left behind.

My grandfather Ité Sįyákhiya had only two sons with my grandmother Turtle Lung Woman. The oldest of their sons is my father, Thathą́ka Ną́žį, Standing Buffalo. Their second son is Sįté, Tail. Standing Buffalo and Tail were the only sons he had with Turtle Lung Woman. It was not that Turtle Lung Woman did not want any more children, it was said that she had a mishap during her childbearing years and she couldn't have any more children. Perhaps that was why she allowed Ité Sįyákhiya to seek other women to have the children she could not.

Ité Sįyákhiya sought women in distant places, where they said he had as many as thirty wives. These women were in other places like Rosebud, Oglala, Parmalee, Red Scaffold, Eagle Butte, and as far away as Montana. The many places where, to this day, they say, he has different families.

Turtle Lung Woman was one of Ité Sįyákhiya's "thawícu." "Tháwa" or "thá" means "belonging to him," "wį" means "woman," and "icú" means "take." The word "thawá'icu" means "to take a woman who belongs to him." It was the way some men saw women back then. In those days, if a man took a woman and paid the price, she was his. He could court her, take her, or if she were from an enemy tribe, capture her.

The word "wi'óyuspe" means "capture a woman." It refers to the ritual of courtship. If a woman did not feel the same way a man did, in those days, he sought the help of a "wóphiye yuhá," a medicine man, one who knew about such things. He asked the wóphiye yuhá for love medicine. The medicine man told him to steal a strand of hair from the woman he loved. He used it to make her suffer with nosebleeds until her family sought help from the medicine man. In that way, the woman was coerced into a relationship with the man. It is said, the love medicine works.

"Líla eháni," a long time ago, "okíchiyuspapi chą," that is to say, "when they held each other," they stood together all night. It was what Ité Siyákhiya had done with Turtle Lung Woman. She remembered how he wore his best buffalo robe and came to her tipi. Her parents consented and allowed him to come. He stood in front of her tipi door, waiting for her. When she didn't come, he paced the ground in front of her door. He did not just walk back and forth, he strode confidently, as if he knew she would eventually come.

When she finally appeared before her door, she stood proudly, in her best buckskin dress. He did not approach her immediately, instead he continued walking in front of her, moving closer and closer to her. When he finally came near, he took her hand and she went with him. He wrapped his buffalo robe around her, and they stood together in front of her tipi door. They stood facing outward, toward the rest of the encampment, but no one looked directly at them. They stood together all night.

A "šíyothąka yuhá," a courting flute, he played for her. It was Itókaǧa, the South Wind, who made the first love flute. Itókaǧa sat at the edge of the world at night and played music with his flute. It created longing in him, he who loved a beautiful young woman.

Itókağa's was the first courting flute. They say it lured the stars to him. These stars became the Milky Way, the pathway from this world to the spirit world, for it was a fallen star Itókağa loved. Her name was Wóȟpe, It Fell.

Turtle Lung Woman remembered how after he had courted her for a while, he came to her father and offered horses for her. She remembered how she felt back then. How she longed to be his, to look upon him as her "hignáku," her husband. "Hí" meaning "he came," "gní" meaning "to go home," and "kú" meaning "to come toward something or someone." So everything in the word "hignáku" referred to him coming home to her.

She stood with him under his buffalo robe all night. The warmth of the fur against her skin, how she felt comforted by his presence and excited at the prospect of sharing his life. They stood all night holding each other. How solid he felt. How she fit under his arm perfectly. How she felt that he would hold no one else that way.

That day he brought home the younger woman, the "ho'íhakakta," the youngest of his wives, Turtle Lung Woman thought she had "wachígnuni," lost her mind, lost her senses. She remembered how it was said that the šíyothąka, the flute, she had heard long ago was also played when the heart was mourning for a lost love. How it could sound as if one were wailing for the dead. How baneful it could sound. How they said it could never be mistaken for the song of the whippoorwill, who calls only for his true love.

The morning she was awakened by the sound of Ité Siyákhiya's footstep and that of his young wife, she saw him as a stranger. Someone she never really knew. As she prepared breakfast for them, Ité Siyákhiya and his young wife, Turtle Lung Woman angrily set down the food. He did not seem concerned by her behavior. This made her even more angry. The other woman looked nothing like she did when she was younger, "owág šíce," she thought, she was not a good-looking woman. This woman did not seem intelligent, with the sense to know that she was not welcome and ought to leave. She sat there and ate the food Turtle Lung Woman prepared.

Turtle Lung Woman said she felt quiet rage welling within her. She said she struggled against herself. She knew Ité Siyákhiya had other sons with other wives but somehow it was more difficult to see it in front of her. She had known about them, these other women, but she never thought that one would come into her house and into her home. She said she could not bear it, so she walked away.

This was allowed in our culture, for a woman to walk away from a man who had been unfaithful. It was even allowed for a woman to beat the man who had been caught having an affair. If she choose to humiliate him, he would not be allowed to defend himself. He could only run away. If he defended himself, he would be the object of ridicule by all. But, this was different. He brought home another wife. He chose to do this and she was to acquiesce and she could not.

It was thought that she had temporarily lost her mind, "wachígnuni," lost her way, when she walked away from her home, away from everything she thought had been hers. She left everything except her medicine bag and her turtles. She would not be allowed to return, in our culture, if she abandoned her home. If she walked away, she would lose all rights to her home and everything in it. She knew that, but she did not care.

She said she would rather go home to her relatives, back to her own people, the Brulé. She walked away from Ité Siyákhiya and his new wife. But as she was leaving she did an odd thing. She put leashes on her turtles and made them walk in front of her, the way one would lead a favorite dog. The turtles walked with her in this manner. How odd they looked, Turtle Lung Woman and her kheglézela, "mániwichakhiye," she made them walk. Slowly they walked up the hill toward the east.

Her family tried to coax her to stay. She did not speak to anyone and instead continued with her turtles toward the east, to the top of the hill, there where the pine trees grew. There she chose a spot by the road and sat down, looking forlornly down at her home. She hid in the shade of the pine trees the entire day, and sat there without food or water.

She stayed there, in one spot. She did not move. She thought about many things that day, up there on the hillside where she sat with her turtles. She did not think good thoughts. Her thoughts were dark and brooding. How appropriate she thought, as she sat looking westward, where Wakíya, the thunder being, lived. She remembered how it was said that Wakíya was a helper too, like Íya, the stone.

She remembered a story about Iktó, the trickster. Her dark thoughts shifted to that story and she could think of nothing else. In the story, she remembered how it was said that Iktó was walking down a road one day. The name "Iktó" is a shortened version of the word "iktómi," or "spider." Iktó was not a spider, but a man who was somewhat deformed. He had a large round body like an insect's, his arms and legs were slender like a spider's, but his hands and feet were large and powerful. It was said that he wore clothes made of buckskin and wrapped himself in a robe made of animal skin. In many ways he was like an ordinary man, but in other ways he was extraordinary.

She remembered how it was said that Iktó was walking down a road one day. As usual he looked hungry but was actively chewing on something. Whatever it was that was in his mouth filled it. He resembled a squirrel with a mouthful of food. Someone asked him, "What are you eating?" Iktó replied, "Nothing." It was clear to anyone watching him that he was indeed eating or chewing on something. Again someone asked him, "What are you eating?" Again, he replied, "Nothing." He suddenly tripped over something on the road and lurched forward, losing his balance. Whatever he was chewing on fell out of his mouth. It was said that Iktó did not want to tell anyone what he was chewing on because he had been chewing on his own "itká," testes. The same way the testicles of a buffalo bull are the choicest part, a delicacy to eat. Iktó ate his "itká."

These were the dark thoughts she had about Ité Siyákhiya and how he reminded her of Iktó. She sat looking toward the west where Wakíya, the dreaded thunder being, lives. She remembered how it was said that he had one offspring, Iktó. She watched the way the sun set, like someone waiting to dive into the water. It looked as if it were perched on the edge of the earth. When the sun finally rolled off the earth, the way the old people said it did, Turtle Lung Woman decided it was best to walk home before it was too dark to see. She picked up her turtles and quickly made her way home.

Customs

Kholápila	Friend
ephé c'ų	I have said
thi'íkceya	in common life
wichóȟ'ą kį	the customs are many
óta yelo	friend
kholá	those
hená éšni yelo	are not it
ephé lo	I have said

7

Lakota Code Of Conduc

I stayed close to Turtle Lung Woman when my n
served her closely, "o'íye nawáȟ'ų," I listened ca
She told me, "Líla eháni, ápa'o ácha," a long time ago, as the light appeared at
dawn, she awakened from sleep and prayed. She greeted the rising sun with
prayer.

Wí, the Sun, is all-powerful and all-knowing, and in its growing light at
sunrise, she prayed with a contrite heart. Wí sees all things, hears all things
spoken or sung, for in the voices of men, women, and children, in the call of
the bird and animal, Tákuškąšką, our Creator, our Lakota God, hears itself.
Tákuškąšką, that which moves, moves, becomes aware of itself. When men
pray or sing, when women pray and sing the tremolo, when children play and
laugh in delight, when the birds, like the meadowlark, sing their morning song,
when Mathó, the great bear, stands on its hind legs like a two-legged and growls
as it attacks, Tákuškąšką moves and lives.

Turtle Lung Woman knew these things. When she prayed, she knew that
she may not have done everything as it should have been done. The way she
was supposed to live fearlessly, speaking only the truth, with a generous heart
and unending patience. How difficult it was to live that way, all of her life.
There were times in her life when she thought it was not possible to be that
way. She knew her humanness, her frailties, and sought Tákuškąšką's pardon,
his patience. "Ómakiya ye," she prayed in the feminine voice, "Help me." She
implored, "Would you help me?" She did not ask for absolution, she asked for
a better way.

"Takúl waglúšna séce," she prayed, "Perhaps I failed in some way." The word
"waglúšna" referred to her awareness, she may have done something unaware,

...ng to. The way we used it the word "waglúšna" meant "I dropped ...ged to me." Indeed it was so, to lose grace. It was something said ...e offended. "Amíkiciktuža ye," in the feminine voice, "Forgive me, my ...r." It meant, "Forget it for me, would you?"

"Wachékiye," she prays. The word "waché," meaning "I cry," and "kiyá," meaning "to send out." So when she prayed, she cried out to Tákuškąšką, that which moves, moves. She sent forth her voice, her cry, her plea to be heard. Her voice was the vehicle for redemption. She spoke. He heard; of that she was sure, for that, she prayed each and every day. "Niyá thą'íyą, wachékiye," with a visible breath she prayed. The cry she sent forth is a feeble one, humble in tone, urgent in need.

In Lakota, there was no such thing as silent prayer, it had to be spoken, to be heard. It had to be sent out. It came from a silent place within. It became a cry sent out, in a single heartbeat, it emerged, it went forth. It was spoken or sung, sometimes both. The way the old people prayed and sang their songs.

Turtle Lung Woman prayed in the early morning with her head bent slightly. Sometimes she raised her hands, the way the people raised their hands and touched the earth as they sat on the ground when the buffalo hunters returned with good news. They raised their hands high in the air and touched the ground in front of them with both hands. She did this as she spoke in a low tone. There was no one present when she prayed, except for Tákuškąšką, that which is in all living things. Her tone was meant for Him to hear. She was sure that He knew these things that she told Him and the things she asked of Him, for Wí was all-powerful and saw and heard all things spoken. All that is unspoken but held in one's heart, He knew as well. She was careful to speak reverently, personally, and in the present tense, for that moment was all that remained in her realm of needs.

A long time ago, when Turtle Lung Woman was young, the people lived a certain way. Just as she knew how to pray at daybreak, she learned to live the way her mother and grandmother lived. A way that required that she remember the code of conduct and abide by it. It had to be so, for her own survival and that of everyone else. There were no written laws, but there were many rules, "wó'óphe óta," many unwritten but known laws that the people lived by. Ordinarily they were never enforced in a punitive way. They were never verbally threatened, "tuwéni šni kį aphé," they never said, "If you do not observe these laws you will be beaten or punished." Yet, they were observed because "eš héchina, héchina, wakháyežala hená ekáš héchųs'e ųspéwichakiyapi chá," that is, throughout time they kept these ways because the children learned the importance of respect. The children were taught very early and very thoroughly.

In the Lakota nation everything began with the family, a man, his wife or wives, and her children. It should rightly be said her children, for they belonged to the woman. "Hená tháwa," it was said of the children, tipí, and almost all of the material belongings of the family, "They were hers." Since the children were her responsibility, most mothers took them and reared them communally with the other women, together, imparting to the children the tribe's values.

In the early days, the younger men were busy hunting or protecting the people against enemy raids, and the women and children remained together at all times. The men stayed clear of the women, especially the young mothers and their children, except to love them, the way most Lakota adults delighted in young children. The men felt responsible for their safety, as they did in protecting the old and infirm. In those days children were considered "wakhá," sacred. Indeed, the Lakota name for them, "wakháyeža," is built on the word "sacred."

The things women were expected to teach and impart to the children were clear and concrete. The skills they needed to teach were the things they did daily and knew by heart. This included everything that needed to be done to keep their households in order. There was no sharing household responsibilities with the men. The duties of the men were clear, they were protector and provider. The women did everything else and more. They too safeguarded the tribe's greatest assets, their children.

They taught certain values to their sons and all the skills required of an industrious wife to their daughters. A son remained close to his mother until he mastered pony riding. Thereafter his friends became his co-conspirators. They watched and imitated the men, their ways quite separate from the women. A girl remained close to her mother most of her life. Both boys and girls loved their mothers and often came to them for reassurance, that is, until puberty. Then, a boy became a man, and his role changed from being defended to becoming protector and from partaking as a child to becoming provider of a nation. A girl, after puberty, prepared for womanhood and her role as mother. It was a virtue, she was told, to have many children.

The other virtues parents were expected to teach were both clear and nebulous. How does one teach bravery, fortitude, truthfulness, generosity, and ultimately, wisdom? It is difficult to teach these qualities valued by the group at an individual level, and even more demanding to live as an example to those under one's care.

Turtle Lung woman knew all too well the frailties of the human spirit. Even so, she assumed her role as mother and everything that it required of her. She saw in her children an extension of herself, of her tribe. Whatever they did reflected on her as mother-teacher, member of her tribe. She saw in the children her own immortality. They would carry her teachings seven generations into the future. It was a daunting task, she had to do her job well.

Turtle Lung Woman did not have many children, she had two sons, Thathaka Nážį and Sįté. She encouraged bravery in her sons. To teach them to live fearlessly, she showed them patience and kindness. She refrained from using harsh language or physical punishment. In this she was no different from other Lakota mothers. If she struck her child she would be a coward, abusing her rightful role as protector of the helpless. If she taught her sons to be cruel, their cruelty would ultimately turn on her. No, it was always better to teach compassion by giving it to children at a young age. Instead, she told them stories about what the appropriate behavior should be. When she spoke to them, she did not refer to them by name. She called them "chį́kš," meaning "son." She never looked directly at her sons, she spoke to them with her eyes averted, and they, too, listened respectfully.

The children learned early to imitate the adults. They learned to distance themselves from others, to disengage, in order to engage in tribal life. They held themselves in check at all times, showing fortitude in all their relationships. They knew by heart these relationships, their family ties. There were clear rules on how one acts toward his or her "até," father, "iná," mother, "kaká," grandfather, "ucí," grandmother, and all of his or her brothers and sisters, each sibling, given a special name according to his birth order. In all these relationships, "kicákaǧipi wayáke," one was expected to show respect.

The children were expected to give and take. They knew it was better to be generous than it was to be selfish and frowned upon, to show fearlessness in play than to be a coward and ridiculed. They knew how proud their parents felt when they told of their achievements and how empty it was to boast and tell lies that no one believed. They knew it was better to face life's challenges boldly than to hide behind Ucí like a small child. These things they learned from listening and observing everyone around them.

Turtle Lung Woman knew that the time she spent with her young sons was short. The time from birth to about the age of four was spent with her. She breast-fed the young boys, who were about four years apart. It was common to breast-feed the child until the age of four, for birth control reasons and for assuring good straight teeth in the child. It was considered poor judgment to have children a year apart. It was thought that children needed proper care and attention, and it would not be possible if they were too close in age.

The time from infancy to early childhood she spent talking and singing to her sons. She was never silent when it came to her children. If they were to value language and thought, it had to begin early. She found herself explaining the most minute detail of life among the people to her young sons, as if the constant and calm way in which she spoke to them would insure that they learned early to do the right thing, in the right way. Thereby avoiding making any mistakes. Though they were small, to her surprise and delight, they learned to listen and listen well. A cradle board helped keep the baby nearby. She spoke to the older one and sang to the younger one. In this way, she kept them close to her. All Lakota women practiced these things, the one virtue they all shared was patience. Their calm and serene way of mothering, equivalent to the fortitude shown by men in hunting and in battle.

The rearing of children was an important occupation for women, just as the sole occupation for men, back then, was that of buffalo hunter. Turtle Lung Woman looked to her mother and grandmother for help and assurance. They knew what it was like and were good-natured in their assistance. They chuckled at the children's attempts to imitate them: the boys hunting small game and watching the men, and the girls watching and imitating them. They stood ready to help Turtle Lung Woman in any way they could. There was never a time when Turtle Lung Woman felt alone, in those early days, at any given moment, the people, especially the women, were constantly together.

She worked with her own sons to teach them these things. Her patience was long with the older one, but the younger one was mischievous and earned the name Sįté, Tail. Her firstborn learned to value these things, including truthfulness and, in time, generosity. Like his name, Thatȟáka Nážį, "buffalo that is standing," he tried to do what was right, what was expected, and became respected among the people. Sįté, on the other hand, was more playful in spirit. His realm was not leadership, as was Standing Buffalo's, but music, dance, and entertainment. He sang well and was respected for it. She had to see these things in her sons and to accept them.

It was what Turtle Lung Woman remembered. She observed her mother and grandmother. She learned from them when she was a child, she remembered everything they taught her, even if at any given moment she could not speak it. It lived inside her and she lived it. I saw it in her. It was a part of her, all that the customs, rules, and ways a Lakota woman should be. She knew even if she couldn't say exactly when or how she learned it. Perhaps as a child she saw her own mother and father behaving a certain way. Perhaps it was the way everyone behaved. Maybe it was in her blood, the memory of the way her people lived all of those centuries.

These things were not written down and were not strictly enforced, yet everyone knew. A look, a whisper, or an uncomplimentary remark aimed at the wrongdoer was all it took to enforce these rules. The code of conduct. The fear of being the subject of such a remark and ridiculed. The fear of being "talked about," and especially after the fact, because then everyone knew what the wrongdoer did and could evaluate it with clear eyes and say that they, under the same circumstances, would not have done it that way. This was all it took to keep these things in everyone's mind – to remember to do the right thing, in the right way.

In time, Turtle Lung Woman embodied all these rules and codes of conduct so that when people looked at her, her own family, all of us, we all remarked at how she stood out. "Ožúla Lakhóta wįyą hécha. Táku echúka," that is, we all said, how remarkable she seemed. The word "ožúla" refers to being full. The way it was used to refer to who she was seemed appropriate. She was fully a Lakota woman in everything she did.

Turtle Lung Woman knew how much effort it took to do the right thing if deep within, at some unconscious level, one really did not want to abide by these strict codes. That was where Iktómi the trickster came in, to keep the inner in line with the outer. Iktómi, whose name meant "spider," was not a spider but a man who was deformed. In all the stories told about him, Iktómi was like a human but in many ways he was an extraordinary being. He, being unusual, tried his best to appear normal and acceptable. He was always at odds with himself. He tried to do the right thing, on the outside, but inside, Iktómi did not always wish to abide by any code of conduct except his own. How transparent and foolish he appeared, Iktómi, the great teacher of what was appropriate.

The stories about Iktómi were many and continued through long winter nights, for it was in the winter that the oyáte in Turtle Lung Woman's time could reflect. They could evaluate all the things they did wrong the previous winter and attribute to Iktómi all the transgressions they may have made. Iktómi was safe – to say that he did it was easier to say than to admit one's foolish mistakes. It was easier to laugh at someone else. Turtle Lung Woman knew that if one listened to the laughter on those winter nights, sometimes one could hear the half-hearted chuckle of one who may have done the same thing only recently.

Two White Buffalo

Ptesą́ Nų́pawį
blihé'ic'iya ų́ wo
oyáte
ókšą
wachį́niyą
a'ú welo
nakénula ya'ų́ welo.

Two White Buffalo
take heart
be strong
the people
around you
depend on you
they are coming
at least
a short time
you
will live

8

Lakota Code Of Conduct – Part 2

Turtle Lung Woman told me many things, including how I was to live and conduct myself according to the Lakota code of conduct. She knew the laws and lived them, so in many ways, it was easy to learn from her. She spoke to me, told me stories, and through her own actions she demonstrated how I was to live and conduct myself as a Lakota woman. The way she spoke was important. I listened carefully to her Lakota words. An important word she used over and over was "wótakuye," which referred to the way I was related to those around me.

In a family, the first child was designated "hokšíthokapha," meaning "the firstborn." The hokšíthokapha in my family was Zįtkála Ská, White Bird. If one was lucky to be the firstborn, one was given special privileges. Zįtkála Ská knew this. He was treated with respect by everyone who knew that he was the firstborn. The birth order of each child is kept track of in a very specific way. My distinction came from the fact that I was "hokšíhakakta," the youngest, and also Wįyą Išnála, Lone Woman, the only daughter in a family of boys.

The way we are related is also kept track of in an exact way. We had to know in what way and remember it. In each family we used terms of address signifying these relationships. In my family, I had many designations indicating my ties to certain family members. My grandparents called me "thakóža," grandchild. They never called me by my name, Wįyą Išnála. They would call me "mithákoža," my grandchild, a cherished term that referred to both male and female.

A grandparent is revered and loved. If a person lives to see two generations, he or she deserves respect. If a person lives to see three or perhaps four generations, he or she is considered sacred. A person's age entitles him or her to respect. It is not only in the way an older person is addressed, it is in the way that person is treated. It has always been that way.

My parents called me "chúkš," daughter. They would refer to me as "michúkši," or "my daughter," when speaking to someone outside the family. When they spoke to me, they would say, "Chúkš," and I would know it was a cherished term used by my mother and father. I distanced myself from my father, out of respect. I remained close to my mother, out of necessity. From her I learned the essential things I needed to know to be a woman. The things she taught me were more practical in nature. The things Turtle Lung Woman taught me about being a woman had to do with the old way. I learned from them both. My mother was a quiet woman and deferred to my grandmother, out of respect. She was often too busy for me. I stayed close to Turtle Lung Woman when I could.

My brothers called me "thąkší," younger sister. They would refer to me as "mithąkši," my younger sister, when they spoke to someone outside the family. In the case of my brothers, however, after a certain age, I never spoke to them directly, but through my sisters-in-law. They never spoke to me directly, out of respect.

In my family alone, I was addressed in many different ways, all signifying my relationship with those around me. I was known fondly as "thakóža," "chúkš," and "thąkáši" or "hąkáši." These names made me feel special as a child. They told me exactly who I was and where I belonged in my family. They also defined how I was to behave toward the person addressing me and how the person speaking should treat me. In other families, these same terms are used in exactly the same way. So that other children like me were called "thakóža," grandchild, or "chúkš," daughter, or "chįkš," son. We Lakotas kept track of such things closely, for such family relationships meant survival in the old days.

I also belonged to a "thiyóšpaye," an extended family, including aunts, uncles, and cousins. They were the people who lived in my community and who were related to me by blood or through a ritual similar to the adoption of a child into a family. They were the people whom I depended on. My thiyóšpaye included many relatives. My female cousins called me "scéphąši." They were indeed my friends. I often chose my female cousins to be my best friends. These women were like sisters to me. My male cousins called me "hąkáši." They were often like brothers to me. My aunt on my mother's side was my second mother, but my aunts on my father's side, I called "thųwį́," aunt. My uncles on my father's side were like second fathers to me, but my uncle on my mother's side I called "lekší," uncle. They in turn called me "thožą́," niece. I felt connected to all of them in my thiyóšpaye. It had to be so, there was no other way to live and survive back then. These were the people who banded together and helped each other through many hardships. These were the people who also came together to celebrate the milestones in my life, my Thathą́ka Lową́pi Wó'echų, or Buffalo Ceremony, and my Hųká Lową́pi, or the Making of Relatives Ceremony. They were the people who knew everything about me.

There were ways in which we were expected to behave toward one another. The words Turtle Lung Woman abhorred were "kağíšnišni," which meant "carelessly." The word "kağí" means "to have regard for someone," and "šnišni" negates the word. So if one acted that way, it meant a lack of regard for someone, or perhaps lack of respect for oneself. "Kağíšnišni wa'échųšni ye," she would tell me, "Do not conduct yourself in a disrespectful way." She expected me to show respect to everyone in my family and extended family.

In all things Lakota, it was not only the word but the thought behind it that mattered. I was taught to listen well. I learned this through my grandmother Turtle Lung Woman. In time I learned that sometimes the spoken word was in conflict with the thought behind it. When this happened I had to respond appropriately, in silence, to say nothing.

In my family, being female, I stayed close to the women in my family, first my mother, then when she was too busy, my grandmother. I learned many things from them. I spent my early years with my mother and after the age of ten with Turtle Lung Woman. She had more time for me, after certain events occurred in her life and she was alone. We were together often and in time I know she depended on me, "wachį́maye," just as "wachį́waye," I relied on her to show me the old way.

I played with my brothers but as we approached the age of ten or so, I no longer played with them, nor did I talk directly to them, unless it was absolutely necessary. I never called them by their names, instead I referred to them as "thibló," older brother. They treated me the same. We never had eye contact when we were in the same room. It was considered inappropriate behavior and showed a lack of regard for that person to do so.

It was said, in my family, that I was headstrong and vocal. My brothers thought this of me, though secretly, and they encouraged these things in me. Or perhaps it was that they tolerated me and allowed me to get away with things I should not have said or done. Perhaps my parents indulged me, being the only daughter they had. I knew what was expected of me, but perhaps I did not always abide by the code of conduct. "Waglúšna séce," perhaps I did things I was not even aware of. In any case, "hél óhą wa'ú," I dwelled there, among them. I was a part of them as they were a part of me. It was the way I remembered it, how appropriate it seemed, to be part of a whole.

The Poor Are Many

Ptesą́ Núpawį̇	Two White Buffalo
waktá yąká yo	watch as you sit
ohų́kešni	be aware
óta ye	the poor
heyápi chą́na	are many
šų́kawakhą	whenever this is said
wéchų we	I donate
	horses

9

Thatȟáka Nážį, Standing Buffalo

Thatȟáka Nážį, whose name meant "buffalo that is standing," or Standing Buffalo, was my father. He was Turtle Lung Woman's firstborn. He was born in the year 1870. What I remember about my father was how my grandmother treated him when she saw him. Their encounters were those of a doting parent and a beloved child. She regarded him with affection and favored him. She bestowed upon him the honor a firstborn deserves.

When I watched Turtle Lung Woman and Thatȟáka Nážį, they reminded me of a story I heard about Stone Boy. In that story it was said four brothers lived alone. One day, one of the brothers stubbed his big toe. It began to swell until it grew quite large. His brothers cut it open and found an infant girl growing inside. They took her and raised her as a sister. She grew into a beautiful young woman. One day, each of her brothers promised her new animal skins to make new things. They left one by one to find game for her. They did not return. She grew sad, and as she was mourning high on a hill, she saw a small round white pebble on the ground. She put it into her mouth and fell asleep. She swallowed the round white pebble and it grew inside her into a child. She gave birth to it, a stone boy whom she loved. She cared for his every need and taught him well.

My grandmother Turtle Lung Woman treated her son the same way. My father, Thatȟáka Nážį, in turn, seemed devoted to her as well. I remember how he would go and see her daily. In the morning he would go and have breakfast with her. He would bring us along, his three younger children. I was the only daughter among them. There were at one time three of us who were his youngest children, all of us two years apart. So, when I was seven years old, my brothers who were closest to me in age were nine and eleven years old. My three older brothers were thirteen, fifteen, and twenty-three years old. The rest of us who were under the age of eleven went everywhere with our parents.

When I was seven years old my grandfather Ité Siyákhiya, Paints His Face with Clay, died and Turtle Lung Woman remarried. She married a man named Mathó Chá Wígni Iyá, meaning "bear goes in the wood." He had been a scout in the U.S. Army and was a fastidious older man. He was the "kaká," the grandfather, I remember. It was said that he had no other family but ours. He treated us well and we were fond of him.

Thatháka Náži, my father, went each morning to his mother's house. He had breakfast there with his mother and stepfather. Turtle Lung Woman and Bear Goes in the Wood lived near us, in her house. It was a one-room log cabin near Phahí Sịté Wakpá, Porcupine Tail Creek. "Hél mayá aglágla," near a ravine, her house stood for many years. Kaká Bear Goes in the Wood received a scout's pension of seventy-five dollars a month and Ųcí Turtle Lung Woman received a pension of fifty dollars a month. "Hená lécha icúb na hél thíb," that was what they lived on.

My father would stop in to see how they were doing and he would take us along with him. I called my father "Pah-pah" and tagged along with the boys when he went visiting. When he came in the morning, Turtle Lung Woman would say to us, "Aphé yąkápi, niyáte wolíglušta kị, yátakte," meaning, "Sit down and wait, when your father is through eating, it will be your turn."

She did not tell us, but it was the way it was done in the old days, when the men ate first, then the women and children. So, when my father sat down upon the deerskin rugs in their house, he was following age-old customs. He sat in the place opposite the door, "chatkúta," the place of honor.

The way Stone Boy's mother thought it best to send him off was with a feast, when he left to find his four uncles. Her four brothers who went to find game for her and did not return. Stone Boy rescued them from Íya the giant. "Íya" means "to complain loudly," an abhorrent trait in our culture. Íya, in our stories, was an evil creature who ate human beings. It was said in the story about Stone Boy that Íya did not eat the four brothers but had flattened them like animal skins and used them to line his tipi wall. Stone Boy's task was to find them and restore them to their normal state.

When Stone Boy left to find them, his mother, who loved him, gave a feast and invited several guests, who brought special gifts for her son. She invited an old woman, who gave Stone Boy a buffalo robe. The old woman painted a dream on the robe, and when he wrapped it around himself he became invisible. She also invited a medicine man, who gave him a "wó'anapte," a protector, to keep him safe. She invited a hunter, who taught him all he knew, and a warrior, who gave him weapons that could defeat any enemy. In short, she gave Stone Boy all the skills a young Lakota man needed to survive in a dangerous world. She invited last, but not least, four beautiful young women, who decorated the buckskins his mother lovingly made for him with mystical things like wolf tracks so he would not grow weary while he searched for Íya's tipi.

When the feast ended, they say Stone Boy promised his mother the safe return of her four brothers. He thanked the three men: the medicine man, the hunter, and the warrior. He turned to the old woman and held high her special robe, signaling how thankful he was. He looked at the four beautiful young women, and he promised to marry them when he returned. They say when he finally departed, after the feast, his mother fell as if she were dead from the grief of his departure.

Turtle Lung Woman and Bear Goes in the Wood reserved the place of honor for her son. They sat on either side of him, on the deerskin rugs. The way people back then preferred to sit upon the ground, close to the earth. She served him broth made from "pápa sáka," or dried beef, and "waštúkala," or dried corn. My father drank the soup with both hands as one would drink water from a bowl. He drank it warm and made loud noises. He did not spill it on himself, but sat quite still. The only movements were in his wrists as he moved the bowl up to his lips and drank like a thirsty horse.

She cut the pápa sáka in small enough pieces so that my father did not need eating utensils. He chewed the pieces well. The pápa sáka takes a while to chew. She set a tin cup of coffee in front of him and he drank his coffee when he finished eating. Turtle Lung Woman had a coffee grinder. She had green coffee beans and knew how to roast and grind them herself. She used the grinder well and knew how to make a strong cup of coffee, the way my father liked it. She boiled water and put the grounds in it. "Wakhályapi," she called it, "heated it is," or "coffee." We also called it "phežúta sápa," or "black medicine." She put "chąhąpi," meaning "boiled from a tree," as maple sugar once was made, so that is what we call white sugar, into the bowl and set it in front of him with a spoon. There my father sat until he finished, between Turtle Lung Woman and Bear Goes in the Wood. We children waited for him. It was the way my grandmother thought it should be.

They say Stone Boy was "wakhą́," or mysterious, because he was not born the ordinary way, from a mother and father. They say his mother was mysterious as well, because she, too, was not conceived the ordinary way. It had to be so, so that they could live forever. Those conceived and born the ordinary way are mortal. Since Stone Boy and his mother were not, they could live forever. It was not so with my grandmother and father, although then and now, they seemed immortal to me.

What I remember about them was the way my grandmother treated her son. The way he expected her to treat him. The way he sat between Turtle Lung Woman and Bear Goes in the Wood, like a young boy sitting with his parents even though he was a middle-aged man by then. The way he treated them, the "wakhą́," the old ones, especially his mother. What I remember the most was how my father drank his soup, how satisfied he seemed. How eager we children were as we waited for our turn.

82

Song in Honor of Ité Sįyą́khiya

Ité Sįyą́khiya	Paints His Face with Clay
ikíchize k'ų	that warrior
waná	now
henákeca ye	is no more

10

Mathó Chą́ Wígni Iyá,
Bear Goes in the Wood

"Kaká," meaning "grandfather," Mathó Chą́ Wígni Iyá, whose name means "bear who goes into the wood," or Bear Goes in the Wood, as he was called in the military, served as a scout in the army. "Kítąla akíchita étkiya o'ų́ye," his ways tended to reflect the influence the military had on him. He leaned toward a soldier's life.

In civilian life, after the military discharged him, Kaká dressed a certain way each day. He wore pants that were like suit pants, a shirt, and suspenders. He followed the ways of the "akíchita," the white man's soldier. In the old days, the word "akíchita" meant something else. A long time ago, that word had a very specific meaning. It signified a Lakota man who was entrusted to keep order and peace among the people. He was required to guard the ways of the people. In those days, the people had no written laws but lived by very strict rules and customs. When it came to maintaining order among the people, the akíchita were respected and obeyed. Kaká, perhaps, liked the idea of being an akíchita, even if it was for a different people.

When he was at home, Kaká wore simple canvas moccasins like Turtle Lung Woman, "hécha ohé," that was what he wore. If he and Turtle Lung Woman were going visiting or to the store they would wear leather moccasins that were beaded in bold geometric designs. They put on their best clothing and groomed themselves well before they went anywhere. They were a handsome couple.

My grandmother was different from Kaká Mathó Chą́ Wígni Iyá: "Ožúla Lakhóta wíyą. Táku echúka Lakhóta étkiya šką́," she was a Lakota woman in every way. There was no doubt as to who she was. In every way, in everything she did, her beliefs in the old ways were reflected. She practiced the old Lakota customs and ways. She followed the old dictates.

Kaká, on the other hand, preferred the new way, the clothes issued to the army scouts, the army pension, and the respect given to the white man's military. The discipline in the army was similar to that required in the old days, before the reservation gradually but certainly changed everyone's life. Kaká liked the life he found in the military until he was discharged. He even shortened his name to "Wood" instead of Bear Goes in the Wood.

Kaká Mathó Chą Wígni Iyá lived with Turtle Lung Woman in her small log house that was built by her first husband, Ité Sįyą́khiya. The house stood north of our house, "mayá aglágla," on a windswept ridge. The back of the house faced the north wind. It had no windows on that side, where the arctic wind blows through the holes in the logs used to construct the house. Kaká periodically put mud between the thick logs to keep the cold wind out.

The front of their house faced ours, we could see their doorway from our house. Although their door was always open, we went only when we were invited to their house. It was within walking distance, but it never occurred to us to barge in on them. "Iyé išnála thípi," they lived alone and independently from us.

Turtle Lung Woman received income each month, what was called an old age pension. "Óta icúpišni eš," that is, it was not much, perhaps fifty dollars a month, but it seemed enough for them. Their needs were not great and the things she and Kaká needed were not expensive, so with their combined income they lived comfortably. "Icíkseya thípi," they were determined to be on their own in every way. "Cha tókhašni é'ųpi," so they lived somewhat carefree. "Héchųs'e o'ų́yąpi na tąyą́ úpi," that was how everyone lived in those days. It seemed like a good way to live.

I felt privileged, as a child, when I was invited into Turtle Lung Woman's house that she shared with Kaká. The things they had in their house seemed special because they were theirs. The cabin itself was small, with dirt floors, and there was nothing unique about it. It looked like all the other small log houses on the reservation. It was a feeling I had about them, their house, and everything they had and did.

The dirt floors in the log house were covered with tanned deer hide rugs. I do not remember a lot of furniture in it. The things I remember are Turtle Lung Woman's bed, which seemed especially inviting and comfortable, and the beautiful blankets that covered the wall behind the bed to keep the draft out. The covered walls and floors made the inside of the house appear gracious. Kaká Mathó Chą́ Wígni Iyá had a rocking chair that I thought was the most wonderful thing they had.

They had trunks in which they kept everything they owned, including their clothing, regalia for dancing, and their different pairs of moccasins. They covered these trunks with tanned deer hide. They had a trunk where they stored certain dried foods. In a large one they kept "pápa sáka," "chąphá," and "waštų́kala," which are dried meat, dried chokecherries, and dried corn. Kaká hammered large nails he bought from the trading post on a cottonwood tree that stood north of their log cabin. There they hung meat that they smoked and dried. It kept well. When the meat was completely dried they stored it in the trunk. When dried this way, it was "sáka," or "very stiff." It was wrapped in paper or a cloth sack and stored in the trunk. "Héchųs'e o'ų́yąpi," that was the way they lived. They were a meticulous people, they took care of the smallest detail with the greatest care. The way Lakota people used to live, in a deliberate way.

One day while Turtle Lung Woman was outside she noticed that one of her dogs had trotted into her house. She heard it bark loudly inside the house. "Tóškhe táku cha?" she wondered out loud, "What is it? What is going on in there?" She followed the dog into the house. She saw it standing near the trunk where she stored food, and suspecting that it wanted the contents of her trunk, she asked the dog, "Tókhiya lá he?" "Where are you going?" She wanted to know. "Kawíǧa ye," she said firmly, "Turn around!" At that moment, Turtle Lung Woman heard frightened cries in the corner of her house. She blinked in the dim light of the cabin. In a dark corner sat a boy around seven or eight years old. She had not noticed him before. He began to cry.

The young boy thought Turtle Lung Woman was speaking to him when she said in a loud voice, "Kawį́ǧa ye." He began sobbing when he thought she had caught him. He thought she had noticed him rifling through her food trunk, looking for pápa sáka. He came into her house, unnoticed, to pilfer choice tidbits of food from the trunk, when the dog saw him and began barking loudly, alerting Turtle Lung Woman. She did not suspect anyone other than her own dog. In her day, there were no thieves. When she saw how miserable the young boy was, she felt sorry for him. She gave him some pápa sáka and sent him home.

There were no lamps to furnish light for them at night. Turtle Lung Woman and Kaká relied on "hawí," the moon, to provide light when they needed it. They lived as they had always done in earlier times before they were put on the reservation. They were getting on in years and they went to bed when the sun went down, "ȟtayétu chą," in the early evening, getting out of bed at the first sign of morning. "Ą́pa'o ácha," when the light appeared at dawn.

They heated their small house with a wood stove. They had a wood pile to the side of their house, where I would sometimes gather wood chips or wood for Turtle Lung Woman. My father chopped wood for them and gathered dry logs to take to their wood pile when he went out to find firewood for the winter. Turtle Lung Woman used it to cook on her wood stove. She made bread, soup, or coffee on the stove top. Their water came from a nearby natural spring. They had everything they needed. "Ešáš tąyą́ úpi, ehą́ni," they lived comfortably back then.

They had horses that grazed on the prairie grass on their land. They tied medicine bundles around the necks of their favorite horses to keep them well. They named those that they loved. Kaká banged on metal pots to bring the horses in. They rose up over the ridge behind the house, neighing and shaking their heads as they climbed up the steeper part of the ravine. When they came in close to the log house, Kaká would give them oats.

He called them in when he was getting ready to go out with Turtle Lung Woman. They traveled to a trading post, a general store five miles south of where their house stood, and along the way they would stop and visit their relatives and friends. When they went visiting, "eháni hená líla ȟ'aȟíya wichó'icaǧe," back then, people like them had a different notion of time.

Kaká hitched up a buggy he had and the two of them would ride together, side by side, to see someone they knew, on their way to the trading post. There is an old wagon trail leading to the store, you can still see it today. It was the old road called Big Foot's Trail, the same road that Chief Big Foot took to his death at Wounded Knee when he and his band of people were massacred there in 1890. Kaká and Turtle Lung Woman traveled that same road, twenty-five years after, to visit their relatives and friends.

They rode together, Kaká and Turtle Lung Woman, side by side, to the trading post. Their horses moved slowly and deliberately: "wichó'icaǧe waštéka," it used to be a good way to live, according to the old way, without the constraints of time as we know them now.

In their day, "líla waká ótapi," there were more older people like them. The elders were more numerous, it seemed. "Hená waká kį," those elders, the way they addressed one another, was always of interest to me. They knew each other by the old names. They used them to identify themselves and did not refer to any English names. They were always glad to see one another. I remember once when I went to see an old friend of theirs. She asked me, "Nitúwe he?" "Who are you?" She wanted to know, her eyesight was dim and she didn't recognize me. "Wíya Išnála, miyé," I replied, "I am Lone Woman." "Kheglézela Chaǧúwį ųcíwaye," I said, in the feminine voice, "I am Turtle Lung Woman's granddaughter."

I watched Ųcí and Kaká as I grew. I did not know that Kaká Bear Goes in the Wood was my step-grandfather. I thought this man, Mathó Chá Wígni Iyá, was my true grandfather, but I was told later that he was Turtle Lung Woman's second husband, whom she married in her seventy-seventh year. In the years that I knew him, he acted like he was my blood relative, my real grandfather, and I accepted him as such. It was the Lakota way, to accept others into one's family this way. Being related to someone was not always through the blood line, but in the way a person acted like he or she was a part of a family. It was not enough to say a person had been adopted into a family, the person had to prove he or she was part of a family, with all the responsibilities that entailed. It included looking out for one another, the way Kaká had always looked after us, and how we regarded him as one of us.

Kaká Mathó Chá Wígni Iyá had no children. "Chicá waníca škhe, na thakó-žakpakula, tákukala" depend "úyapi," since he had no children, and thus, no grandchildren, it was us, Turtle Lung Woman's family, who became his family. We were interdependent, all of us. He was our Kaká, the grandfather I knew and loved. It was the way I remembered it. It was the way I wished it would remain.

Then, on January 30, 1930, Kaká Mathó Chá Wígni Iyá died. I was ten years old then but I remember how sad I felt when Kaká died. He had been sick for a while and some of our relatives came to camp near their cabin, hoping he would get well. When he died everyone we knew came for the funeral. Some of them brought white canvas tents and camped nearby. They brought everything they needed and stayed two nights and three days in that cold February weather, in the month we call Chanáphopa Wí, or Moon of the Popping Trees, when it is so cold the trees crack and fall from the ice.

In those days they did not embalm them, so they kept him for a short time. They had a two-night wake. All of the relatives stayed awake, crammed into Turtle Lung Woman's small cabin. They had the funeral on the third day. The ground was frozen but somehow they dug a grave and buried him in it on the hillside at St. Julia's Episcopal Church. In very severe winters they had what was called a cadaver house near the trading post, and they kept bodies there until it was easier to dig the frozen earth to bury the body. I don't remember Kaká being kept there.

He had been a scout, so the government gave him a gravestone. The stone stood about five feet tall. It looked like a pillar pointing upward to the sky, the way Kaká had been to me, a source of strength. It is still there on the hillside at St. Julia's, the white stone, weathered by time. On the gravestone, it reads, "Bear Goes in the Wood." In the old days, an honoring song would have been all that was left of Kaká, for we Lakotas did not erect monuments to the dead. A scaffold would have been erected back then. A scaffold made with four young trees with their branches reaching upward to the sky. On the branches would be made a bed for him to lie on with his face to the sky. He would be covered with a robe and a webbing made of young branches bent over him. He would stay there on the scaffold while the winds blew from Waziyata, the north. His spirit would return home along the Milky Way, in the night sky. They would have sung his song, "Mathó Chą Wígni Iyá, ikíchize k'ų, waná henákeca ye," "that warrior, now, is no more."

After he died, Turtle Lung Woman lived alone. She buried two husbands and thereafter chose to be alone. "Ųcí išnálala eš, héchenaš hél thí," although Grandmother was now alone, she still lived as she had with Kaká Mathó Chą Wígni Iyá. We knew she missed him, the way we all did. She was eighty years old, living there as she had always done.

My father would often check on her, to see how she was getting along. He respected her need to be alone, to be independent as she had always been. "Táku hená iyé ilágye," she relied on her old age pension to support herself. She seemed content living that way. When she wanted to travel to the trading post, she had a horse-drawn buggy that she hitched. "Iyé iyáglaškį na iyá," she tied on the horses herself and away she went.

"Waníyetu óta," she was many winters, but she still did everything on her own. She conducted her life as if time did not weigh on her, the way it had on the men she had married. The men she had been faithful to. In time they fell ill and died, while she lived. How strong she seemed. She was not frail in any way. Her hair was still dark, there was no hint of gray in it. Her eyesight was failing somewhat and her hearing was not what it had been. She did not seem at all worried about these things. In her cabin by the ravine, she seemed content. Her life continued on a while longer after Kaká died. I was glad for that time, for the opportunity to be with her, now that she was alone.

Honoring Song

Khuwápe	They pursued him
théhą	a long
khuwápe	time
Khąǧí kį	the Crow men
khuwápe lo	pursued
Khąǧí kį	him
nážįyąpi	the Crow men
théhą	surrounded him
khuwápe	a long time
Khąǧí kį khuwápe lo	they pursued him

11

"Akhé Iktó," Again, Iktómi, the Trickster

When Turtle Lung Woman, my grandmother, wanted to tell me a story about Iktó, she would say, "Akhé Iktó echá," meaning, "That Iktó, he was at it again!" She always began her stories this way. I learned to listen well, for it was in these stories that I learned how not to act. If I listened well and didn't do what Iktó did, I would be wiser. Ųcí always ended these stories promising to continue the next night if I went to sleep. These stories were never told during the day, if someone asked for a story during the day, they had to pay for it, it was said, with a special payment or gift.

Turtle Lung Woman told these stories in the night, in the darkness when it was bedtime for me. Indeed the darkness of a winter night seemed like the best time to tell these stories. In the old days storytellers told these through the length of a winter camp when the people stayed primarily indoors. They say long ago we made our "wanáthipi," our winter camps, east of the river we called Mníšoše, or "muddy water," the name we gave to the Missouri River.

"Akhé Iktó echá," she would begin, and I would find a comfortable spot to lie while she began her story in an amused voice. The name she used, Iktó, is a shortened version of the word "iktómi," which means "spider." Iktó was not a spider, but a man who was deformed. His body was big and round like an insect's; his arms and legs were slender like a spider's; but his hands and feet were large and powerful. He wore clothes made of buckskin and wrapped himself in a robe made of raccoon skin.

In many ways he was like an ordinary man, but in other ways he was extraordinary. Iktó was "wakhá," in the sense that he was mysterious. It was said that he came into being as Ksá, meaning "wise," but became Iktó, the foolish. It was Iktó who uttered the first human words and invented language. He was created first and saw everything else being created, and he named all things. He could communicate with everything including stones, plants, animals, and spirits. He could speak to Wakíyą, his father, the winged creature. It was said that Iktó was Heyókha, the one who paints his face black to show that he was rejoicing. Iktó was both mysterious and ordinary, perhaps like all human beings.

He enjoyed the same things human beings did, the company of others. He delighted in playing jokes on everyone. He would fool men, spirits, and anything else that he came across that he could communicate with, to get what he wanted from them. He would lie if it helped him, but if you lied to him, he would play tricks on you. He would cheat if it meant that he would win, but if you won he could make you do foolish things to look ridiculous.

So, when Ųcí began her story, "Akhé Iktó echá . . ." in an amused voice, I knew it was time to take a good look at Iktó. It was time for a story. One day Iktó was walking somewhere, again. Then he noticed an "íya" sleeping. An íya is a giant creature. As it lay sleeping it looked like a small mountain moving up and down. Its breath shook the earth. It is said that Íya often travels with Iktómi, for they are both "wakhą́," or "mysterious." Íya is more dangerous because he is evil.

So it was that Iktó saw him sleeping. Iktó knew that if Íya woke up he might eat him, for Íya eats everything, including human beings. As he stood there watching Íya sleep he decided to outsmart the giant. He stood deep in thought. He woke Íya. "Kiktá yo," Iktó said in the masculine voice, "Wake up." "Léchiya blá cha ųyį́kte," he said to Íya, "I am going over there, so you can come with me." Upon hearing this, Íya jumped up and began breathing even louder, and in doing so, he pulled at Iktó with his breath. Íya's breath was so strong that that Iktó looked as if he might become Íya's next meal. Íya was so large that Iktó looked like a fly next to him. Íya looked like he was about to pull Iktó in each time he breathed in!

"Áta léchel niyá," Ųcí would say, "he breathed like this." She would make a loud breathing noise like she was short on breath and moved her chest up and down to show how Íya must have looked as he woke up and stared at Iktó. Iktó, rightly so, became afraid of Íya. To mask his fear, he said loudly, "What if I, too, inhaled and pulled you in my mouth?" "Yamáhe échiyayįkta," Iktó said, "I could gulp you in too!"

"Héchegla gnáyą," Ųcí would say, "It did not take much to fool Íya." He believed Iktó had the capacity to eat him. Afraid, Íya addressed Iktó by a kinship term, "chiyé," meaning "older brother." Íya deferred to Iktó as a respectful younger brother would. Iktó took the lead, satisfied that he had deceived Íya.

Iktó, in turn, addressed Íya, referring to him by the kinship name "misų́," younger brother. He asked, "Misų́, níš táku khoyákipha he?" "Younger brother, tell me, what are you afraid of?" Íya told Iktó that he was most afraid of three things: "Wagmúha, chácheǧa, na šíyothąka. Chiyé, hená khowákipha," he said to Iktó, "Older brother, I am afraid of these." The things he named were a rattle, a wooden kettle or drum, and a flute. Íya was afraid of the loud noises these instruments made. Iktó told Íya that he too was afraid of the same things.

Then Iktó said to Íya, "Misų́, lél oyáte wichóthi cha él ųyį́kte." He told him, "Younger brother, there is a village nearby so we will go there." Together, they began walking in the direction of the camp. By then, Íya was hungry and he was happy to hear that people were nearby so he could eat them all.

When they were near it, Iktó turned to Íya and said, "Tųwéya mníkte," saying that he would go quickly and see what was ahead. Iktó said he would spy on the camp and report back to Íya. He told Íya to sit and wait for him while he went ahead.

When he reached the village, Iktó warned the people, "Íya wą kichí wa'ú," he said, "I am coming with a giant." He told the people, "Táku lená khokíphe," that the giant was afraid of these things, and he told them what to bring. He told them to bring their rattles, drums, and flutes. "Kichí thiwégna wahíyu kį," he said, "When you see us walk through the village, among the tipis," then make as much noise as you can with the things he is afraid of. So, the people sent out a crier through the camp and prepared themselves to meet Íya, the giant. "Wíyeya nážipi," they stood ready.

Iktó returned to where Íya sat waiting, "Ho, Misú," he said, "Now, little brother," and led him toward the village. Iktó told him that it was a large camp and asked if perhaps Íya wouldn't mind dividing the village in half so that they could both enjoy a great feast. "Wichúyutįkte," he said, "We will eat everyone."

When they reached the outskirts of camp, everyone there was ready with all the things that Íya told Iktó he was afraid of. Suddenly they pounced on Íya with all the noisemakers: shaking their rattles, beating furiously on their drums, and blowing their flutes loudly.

"Ȟláȟla kį wa'ícakakapi na cȟácȟeǧa kį kabúpi na šíyotȟaka kį yažópi na awíchaš'api," they shook their rattles, beat their drums, and blew their flutes, yelling as loudly as they could. Íya fainted with fright. As soon as Íya fell to the ground, the men jumped on him and cut him open. It was said that when they did, all the people and creatures he had eaten came out of him. They were all set free.

Ųcí would then say, "Hųhé, wicháša wą chąpágmiyąpi wą ogná hinápha škhe," it was said that a man on a wagon emerged from Íya! I would laugh, knowing it was the end of the story and Ųcí was only exaggerating.

There were other stories about Iktó that Ųcí had told me. The story about how Iktó fell in love with his mother-in-law. How ordinary his wife looked, but how his mother-in-law was quite beautiful. Iktó desired her to be his woman and thought about how he could make this happen. After thinking a while, Iktó decided that he would announce to his wife that he was going on a war party and he needed his mother-in-law to come with him to make his moccasins.

So, Iktó and his mother-in-law departed. After they had been gone for a long time, everyone thought that the enemy had killed them. One day, many years later, while they were looking for buffalo, the people came upon a tipi in a small clearing. There were small children playing around the tipi as they approached it. As they came near, who should emerge from the tent but Iktó and his mother-in-law! Although it was obvious that Iktó had made her his woman and that the children playing outside were theirs, Iktó acted surprised to see the children. "Lená khaǧí wakháyeža kį khigléwicha'ųyąpi škha," he said, "These are children of our enemy, the Crow. We captured them and decided to set them free. But they keep coming back." Iktó shouted loudly at the children. He ran toward them as if to scare them away.

Although they were his own children, Iktó was so afraid that they would see the terrible thing he had done in taking his mother-in-law that he ran after the children. He picked up a small stick and chased them away. How ridiculous he looked, his big belly hanging to the ground, running after them. Uçí would shake her head, "Akhé Iktó echá . . ." He was at it again.

The Many Lands You Fear

Kholá,
óte makhóche wą
khoyákiphapi
hená khokíphešni omáwani
ité isábye cha
owále

Friend
the many lands
you fear
in them without fear
I have walked
the black face paint
I seek

12

"Blihé'ic'iya Wa'ṵ," With Dauntless Courage, I Live

Turtle Lung Woman knew the old ways because she was born at a time when things were still steeped in the old ways. They were changing but at a slower rate than when I was born. I was born in 1920, by then she was sixty-nine years old, and the world was changing daily.

Turtle Lung Woman was born in 1851. In the winter counts this was the year a treaty council met with the "wašícu," or "white men," at the fort near Laramie River. It was the winter when "wakpámnipi tháka," when many things were given to the people. In return for these many things he gave, the wašícu was slowly taking more and more of our lands.

These lands stretched from central South Dakota southwest into Nebraska along the Phąkéska Wakpá, meaning "shell river," or the North Platte River. This "wakpá," this river, set the southern boundary of our hunting territory. In the northwest the Powder River, running along the Bighorn Mountains into Montana, set another natural boundary. These lands continued north along the Powder River through the southeastern tip of Montana into North Dakota. They covered the western half of the state of South Dakota. The Mníšoše Wakpá, meaning "muddy river," the Missouri River, set an eastern boundary for us.

There were "thóka," or "other people," who lived near us. The Hidatsa lived north of our lands in what is now North Dakota. The Ȟewáktokta, the Arikaras, lived east of us in South Dakota. The Phaláni, the Pawnees, lived to the southeast in what is now central Nebraska. The Šahíyela, the Cheyennes, our friends, lived southwest of us in what is now southern Wyoming. In the west, where the dreaded thunder beings lived, the Khągí wicháša, the Crows, had their lands.

It was a vast area of land that was ours. "Lakhota ų ektá," we say, "where our people dwelled." We hunted the buffalo there. In time these lands were taken and we were told we could no longer hunt. Turtle Lung Woman saw the people give up these lands. She learned how to make moccasins out of canvas instead of buffalo hide. The buffalo were our lifeline. Once that was cut, we could no longer survive on our own. We could no longer define our world based on "thathąka," the buffalo. Instead, Thathąka Gnaškíyą, Crazy Buffalo, from our stories and myths, appeared and remained among us. Its spirit was evident in everything the wašícu did. The wašícu came, appearing to be at times generous, promising many things. The way Crazy Buffalo deceives the unwary.

In time the wašícu persuaded Lakota men to do things that were not in the best interest of the people. The way he convinced them that treaties would be honored, nation to nation. The way he used these same treaties to take away everything that was good in our lives, our way of life. They say Crazy Buffalo is the most dreaded of all. They say he is the most evil being because he deceives so cruelly.

Turtle Lung Woman, as an adolescent, heard of Thašųka Witkó, "his horse is wild," or Crazy Horse, who refused to sign any treaty. She heard of Maȟpíya Lúta, or "cloud that is red," Red Cloud. How he signed some treaties. How one man listens to his heart and the other to Crazy Buffalo.

She grew up hearing about these leaders. She was fifteen years old when all the land west of the Mníšoše Wakpá, the Missouri River, was made into a reservation for the Lakota people. At the time Red Cloud traveled to Washington DC to talk to President Grant about the hardships faced by the people, she was seventeen years old.

Turtle Lung Woman was twenty-three years old when the government finally ordered the people to live on reservations. She had been married for five years. She had given birth to two sons by then.

It was then that the people were camped at Greasy Grass, known as Little Bighorn, where Custer died. They did not camp there to kill. They were gathering there as they always did at that time of the year. It was Custer who came with ill intent and surprised the people.

In 1879, when the Pine Ridge Reservation was finally established for the Lakota people, she was about twenty-eight years old. She had lived among these men, Crazy Horse, Sitting Bull, and Red Cloud. When Sitting Bull fled north into Canada, and Crazy Horse was murdered, she heard what happened to them when they were arrested. As she feared, the spirit of Crazy Buffalo roamed the land, unimpeded. He ruled. He persuaded the people to murder each other. He was indeed evil.

When the Ghost Dance was brought from the Paiute tribe in 1889, Turtle Lung Woman was nearing middle age. When two hundred men, women, and children were killed at Chąkpé Ópi, Wounded Knee, in 1890, she heard of the "wanáǧi," the ghosts, that frightened the dogs and made them bark all night. She lived through these events, and finally, when Red Cloud died in 1909, Turtle Lung Woman was over fifty years old. She had been practicing as a medicine woman.

"Iwíchawahąble," the dream she had about the íyą remained vivid in her mind. When she remembered it, she knew how to help people. She knew how to use the medicinal herbs. She knew how to conduct the Yuwípi, or the Binding Ceremony, in which the turtles walked to help free her. The "kheglézela," the turtles, those ancient small creatures as old as time, walked the way the people used to walk "líla ehą́ni," way back when.

The Yuwípi, for her, as it was throughout time, was a ceremony using "íyą," or "sacred stones," to help others. She first heard the íyą speak in that first dream she had.

It told her his name, Wó'anapta, meaning "protector." It was the same íyą who came and asked her to be its eyes, hands, and feet. She agreed to everything he said. She knew he meant no harm. He had said she would be a healer. He said she would have the ability to travel into the future, and her vision would be clear so that she would return to her people and tell them what she saw.

It was not until she had been practicing as a "Yuwípi wíyą," a Yuwípi woman, that she remembered. In her dream when the íyą came to her she had seen a vision. In it she saw an effigy of Thathą́ka Gnaškíyą, Crazy Buffalo. It hung from a sacred pole in a Sun Dance. It was painted black to signify that he was dead.

PART 2

Lone Woman
(Wį́yą Išnála)

Children's Lullaby

Awawawa	Awawawa
iníla istį́mala	quietly sleep
awawawa	awawawa
iníla istį́mala	won't you
awawawa	be still
iníla istį́mala	awawawa
awawawa	quietly sleep
iníla istį́mala	be still
	awawawa
	won't you

13

Raised on Canned Milk

"Líla eḩani," a long time ago, it was thought that certain spirits were appeased only when a woman became pregnant. They plagued her throughout her child-bearing years. They made her bleed each new moon until she became pregnant, then they left her alone for a while. When she became pregnant, she gathered wood from the cottonwood tree and kept a small bundle of sticks from this tree near her to ward off the dreaded Anúg Ité, the Wíy̧a Núpapika, the Double Faced Woman.

Anúg Ité's face was split down the center. One side reflected her former self, a vain and beautiful young woman, and the other side reflected her true self, a tormented, hideous creature. Her split face was her punishment for being un-faithful to her husband, Thaté, Wind. As further punishment she was banished from her home and stripped of her maternal rights.

Anúg Ité had four sons, who later became the four sacred directions. They were quadruplets. Each son was put in charge of a specific direction, west, north, east, and south. Anúg Ité was pregnant with her fifth son when she was punished for seducing another woman's husband. Her unborn child was taken from her. This child, because he was premature, would always be weak and small. His name was Thaté Oyúmni, Little Whirlwind, the son of Thaté. He is that small wind out on the prairie that kicks dust in your eyes. The small wind that rises from nowhere and attacks itself and dies into nothingness. Anúg Ité decided that because she was deprived of her pregnancy and could not carry her son to term, she would henceforth torment pregnant women and babies.

Turtle Lung Woman said when a woman became "iglúš'aka," meaning "she strengthens herself," it meant that she was with child. The spirit of the buffalo, it was said, was always pleased to see a woman with child. He would help her if she was not lazy or lewd. She had to take certain precautions to ensure a full-term infant who would grow strong and healthy. She was told to take early-morning walks. It was thought that the fetus would grow strong, encouraged by the first light of dawn. In the nine months of her pregnancy she tried hard not to look too long at any odd thing, any unusual-looking animal or person, for fear that her child would be deformed in some way.

When she was in labor, it was called "hokší wazápi," meaning "a child, in pain, she will bear." It was thought that Anúg Ité, Double Faced Woman, was responsible for this suffering. She delighted in bringing misery to human beings, especially women. When a woman gave birth, it was called "hokší yuhá," meaning "a child she has." She did so in her own tipi, in the presence of a trusted female relative who knew about midwifery. If she had problems during childbirth, a "phežúta wíyą," a medicine woman, like my grandmother Turtle Lung Woman, was summoned.

They came for Turtle Lung Woman regardless of the time. Indeed it seemed that most infants came when the moon was full. The full moon was called "wí mimá," round moon. It helped us keep track of time and the changing seasons. Our years are counted by the winter. In a year there are thirteen moons and four seasons. The thirteen moons appear as two moons in "wétu," in springtime; four moons in "blokétu," which is the summer; two moons in "ptąyétu," autumn; and four and sometimes five moons in "waníyetu," in winter. The Lakota year begins right after the last winter moon, in the first moon of spring. Magáksica Aglí Wí, it is called, The Moon When the Ducks Return. We did not keep a written history but certain men kept winter counts, pictographic recordings of important events that occurred each winter.

We called the moon "hąhépi wí," or "night sun."

In our stories, it was Hąhépi Wí whose husband Anúg Ité tried to seduce. The moon's husband, Wí, Sun, was told that for his acquiescence he would forever lose his companion, Hąhépi Wí. She would hide her face in shame. Only when she was far from the sun would she show her face. It was then that the two times were made, night and day. Wí travels alone across the sky during the day, and Hạhépi Wí journeys alone at night. Hạhépi Wí's energy is female, her spirit benevolent. Wí's energy is male, his spirit benign.

It is under her gentle light that most "wakháyeźala," the "little sacred beings," journey to this world. When they summoned her, Turtle Lung Woman would take her medicine bag to attend to the woman in labor. A pheźúta wíyạ like Turtle Lung Woman was usually older, beyond menopause. She who had the power to nourish and make grow. She was past the monthly bleeding, that mysterious and dreaded time that women endured. She was free of it and far from childbearing.

The reputation of a pheźúta wíyạ like Turtle Lung Woman depended upon her character, how well she had raised her family, how industrious she was, and how well she got along with others. If she was to be present at a birth, the parents of the infant wanted assurance that she was a virtuous person, for with her touch she would transfer her character to the newborn infant.

Turtle Lung Woman knew all of these things when she helped at childbirth. "Ówichakiya," we say, "she gave assistance to the women." She witnessed many births and knew what to do if anything went wrong. Her small deft hands delivered many babies. She herself had only two children, yet she delivered many. She delighted in hearing the muffled cry of the newborn. "Ho hé," she would say, "It is good," as she cleared the infant's airway at birth. Turtle Lung Woman was a good woman. When she touched the infant, she could only bestow what she was.

The women were expected to show forbearance, dignity, and self-control during childbirth. "Líla ehạni," a long time ago, they did not lie down during labor but knelt on the ground. A wooden stake about three feet tall was driven into the ground. When the last stages of labor began, the woman knelt at the stake and held on to it while she gave birth in an upright position, relying on something as natural as the force of gravity to help her during the most difficult time. When the newborn finally emerged, the attending midwife held a piece of soft deerskin to catch and hold the infant.

In those days women bit a knife to show they were speaking the truth. Likewise, in childbirth they were expected to show fortitude. When the child is born, we say "hokší yuhá," meaning "a child she bears." The other women present during the birth compliment her on her bravery. Indeed, she had to be. She had to keep her wits about her when she knelt at the stake during the last stages of labor to give birth. "Tąyą́ echánu," they would say to her, "You did well."

Turtle Lung Woman or the midwife present would take the umbilical cord and sever it about three inches from the infant's stomach. She would take dry spores from a fungus and put it on the navel where the cord is newly cut, to foster proper healing. She would take a soft clean strip of deer hide and tie it at the end of the cord to keep it in place. When it fell off, usually within four days, the mother put it into a small pouch. She did this "hená tąyą́ icáǧapikta cha," so that her child would grow strong and be of firm character.

She made two pouches, one in the shape of a turtle to ensure long life. The other was made in the shape of a lizard to ward off the dreaded Anúǧ Ité, who delighted in making newborns miserable with stomach and bowel ailments. The umbilical cord was kept in the turtle-shaped pouch. The lizard-shaped pouch was kept as a decoy for certain bad spirits that could harm the wakháyežala, the small sacred being.

Turtle Lung Woman said that sometimes the pouch was attached to a longer piece of leather cord, and the child wore it like a necklace. It was decorated with beautiful quillwork or beadwork and it was sometimes hung from a tipi wall. "Iyé gluhápi," that is, the person for whom it was made kept it. "Thewíchaȟilapi," they did this for the children they cherished. If this was not done properly it was said that the child would spend his life searching for his umbilical cord. "Chekpá okíle séce," they would say of him, "Perhaps he was searching for his umbilical cord."

She helped the mother expel the afterbirth. She took it, wrapped it properly, and tied it high in a tree. She did this so that the coyote would not take it and bring disgrace to the woman. The spirit of the coyote was malevolent and wished harm upon women. It brought only sadness and sorrow where it went. Iktómi, the trickster, was a friend of the coyote. He rode upon him. The spirit of the coyote did the bidding of Anúg Ité, Double Faced Woman. It was said that if a coyote took the afterbirth, the woman would grow lazy and do disgraceful things, bringing shame to her family. The spirit of the buffalo would not help her. The afterbirth was never buried in the ground for fear that it would invite death for the newborn.

On the fourth day after giving birth, the woman was purified. "Azílwicha-yapi," she was cleansed with water mixed and boiled with leaves from the sage plant. An older woman relative helped her by bathing her gently with a soft deerskin cloth dipped in the sage water that was cooled to lukewarm. "Pakhítapi," she was wiped clean. Once she was purified, she was free to resume her life as before. "Kiktápi," she awakened or arose from rest, ready to resume her life. Until she was purified she remained still.

The woman rested for four days after the birth of her child. She kept the infant near her, nursing it while she rested. "Azíkhiya ye," so the new mother is en-couraged, "Let the infant suck at the breast." She fed it immediately after the birth, the baby was put on her stomach and the wakháyežala stared wide-eyed at the mother, its dark eyes alert and curious. The world the wakháyežala saw was a Lakota world filled with order and meaning.

The wakháyežala, the little newborn, was gently cleansed with tepid water that had been boiled with dry sage leaves. A soft deerskin was used to wipe the baby. Then buffalo fat was rubbed upon its skin. Sometimes, the infant was symbolically painted red with ocher to signify that he or she is from the "pté oyáte," the buffalo calf people. The ocher kept the baby's soft skin from drying out. The wakháyežala was swaddled in soft deerskin and never left uncovered or alone. It remained close to her.

A Lakota wakháyežala was born with dark birthmarks down its lower spine. The dark spots were about the size of a nickel and disappeared after the first year. The wakháyežala had down-like hair on its shoulders and back that would eventually disappear after the first twelve months. When it grew into adulthood, he or she would not have facial hair or any other hair on his or her body other than that in certain private areas of the body and on his or her head.

"Wichágluhapi," the wakháyežala remained close to the mother, relying on her breast milk for the first few years of life. Turtle Lung woman said most wakháyežala were breast-fed for a long time, sometimes throughout the first three years. There was no hurry to wean the infant. The mother nursed as long as she had milk, which could last four years.

A pacifier was made for the baby after six months to help the mother when she was too busy to nurse. The pacifier was made from the ligament of the buffalo. It is a tough piece, from the muscle or tendon, that the mother boiled and used for a pacifier. Turtle Lung woman and the other older women thought this type of pacifier, combined with breast-feeding for a long time, was good for the child's teeth. These things would help the child's teeth grow straight and strong.

The Lakota mother wrapped the infant in soft deerskin blankets to keep it warm, covering its head in a small soft tight-fitting cap similar to a baby bonnet. She did everything in her power to ensure the well-being of the wakháyežala. "Hokšík'į," we say, "she carried her small child in a cradle board." "K'į" refers to the pack she carried on her back with the baby in it. When the wakháyežala was a few weeks old, the mother put her into this soft deerskin pouch, no different from the soft womb that had been baby's home for nine months. It gave the wakháyežala a sense of security, being swaddled and laced into this soft pouch, attached to a wooden frame that the mother carried on her back. The cradle board freed her to do the work necessary to maintain her home.

The cradle board was made by a sister of the father. It was an object of art if it was well made, with the leather portion elaborately decorated with the finest quillwork or beadwork. Sometimes the wood frame was decorated as well. It was equal in value to one horse. A woman did not usually make her own cradle board but accepted one as a gift from a relative. Sometimes she received many, a sign that her child was loved and cherished by many relatives.

The cradle board gave the women mobility. In times of movement from one camp to another it could be tied to a travois or a saddle on a horse. These Lakota saddles became models used by the wašícu, the white man's army. The Lakotas used them earlier in time on their horses. When the people were camped, the women propped the cradle boards upright near their work area. Even then the babies were never ignored. Turtle Lung Woman said the women constantly spoke or sang to their small children. "Eš iyúha tąyą icágapi," most children grew well because they were loved.

I had the distinction in my family of being the "hokšíhakakta," or "the last child," born to my mother. When I was born my mother was close to forty. Because she was older and I was her youngest, I did not have the opportunity to see her in labor. "Ináwaye kį wayázą cha slolwáyešni," I did not see my mother give birth.

When she gave birth to me she did so in a camp ground at Tháȟca Wakpála, Deer Creek. "Waší ųthípi," my father and mother were camped there while they worked in the farm fields in Nebraska. They were there to cut hay for the farmers. My father called it "phežícaǧapi," meaning "making grass," for the white farmers.

The town of Tháȟca Wakpála had a stable at the northern edge of town where my father, Thathąka Nážį, boarded his horses. A campground near it allowed families coming from the reservations to camp there for short or long periods of time. Some families lived there all year long. We only lived there between jobs in the summer months while my father worked in the nearby fields. He had just finished working near Mní Tháka, meaning "large water," which was our name for the Niobrara River, when my mother went into labor.

"Wichóškį'ic'iye," my mother created quite a stir in the campground at Tháȟca Wakpála when she went into labor. She was older and had a difficult time giving birth. My paternal and maternal grandmothers were both there.

Sįté, my father's brother, was there with his wife. Turtle Lung Woman came into the tent, where my mother lay on soft blankets on the ground, with the other women who were gathered in that small space, to help my mother. "Líla wayáza," she was in great pain. She had a hard time with me. They used "Lakhól phežúta," traditional medicine, to help her.

It was then that old man Bull Tail came and prayed for us, my mother and me. "Iná mayúhapi," I was born right there. It was the twenty-fifth day of August, the month we call Chaphásapa Wí, The Moon When the Chokecherries Turn Black, in 1920, the year I was born. My mother was close to forty, her body ached with rheumatism, and she was unable to produce milk for me. "Azímakhiya okíhišni," I was not able to suck milk at her breast.

A long time ago it was said that one of the most difficult things a Lakota man faced was when he lost a wife who was still nursing a child. How hard it was to raise a motherless infant who needed her mother's milk. How the man depended upon other women to help raise his motherless child by donating breast milk to the infant. The women usually did so willingly, knowing the survival of the baby depended upon them as well. Those days were gone by the time I was born. My father went to a wašícu doctor, a white man, and asked him what he could do for me. The doctor told him to give me "pté niní asápi," or "cow's milk."

The "asápi," the milk, my father bought at the store in Tháȟca Wakpála came from a tin can. The can had a picture of a fat wašícu baby on it. The label read "Eagle Brand Milk: There Is a Place in Every Home for Condensed Milk." It was the first time anyone in our family was given "canned milk." My mother did not have any of her own for me. I must have cried long and hard for her milk. How difficult it is to comfort a hungry and unhappy newborn. My father and mother did the best they could.

The label read "Clean Cow's Milk Mixed with Pure Sugar Cane." It was the "Purest, Safest, and Most Nourishing Milk" that they could buy for me. I know now that my mother's milk would have been better for me. The canned milk they gave me made my bones weak.

Song Concerning Fierce Face

Ité Hįyáza
nayáphe cį lo
nithákholapi k'ų
onílotape lo

Fierce Face
do not
flee
your friends
have
borrowed
your soul

14

"Wichį́calala," Small Girl

Our Lakota word for a young girl was "wichį́cala." "Wį́" means "woman," and "chįcá" signifies "her child." A young girl was considered a "woman's child." Indeed she was under the mother's care until she reached puberty. "Íše wį́ya iyéchel khuwáb," my grandmother Turtle Lung Woman said, "A young girl was given the same deference a grown woman received from others in the tribe."

A mother was expected to "speak" to her daughter, to tell her everything she needed to know to survive in the world. "Wókhiya k'úb," she was spoken to not in a negative way, but in a way that taught her what she needed to know.

A mother was expected to reinforce in her daughter the values shared by the women of the tribe. Some of these were taught by the grandmothers and aunts. They knew best the virtues deemed worthy of a Lakota "wį́ya": to be generous, brave, truthful, and, in time, to bear children. This was the greatest virtue of all, to have many children and to be good to them.

"Wį́ya hé tháwa, wį́ya waží yuhá hą́ta," the daughter "belonged" to the mother. She was in essence her mother's property, and therefore her responsibility. The mother had supreme authority over her daughter. Likewise, if she had a son, it was the same, until his voice changed at puberty, then he became the responsibility of his father. "Hé tháwa," or he "belonged" to his father. "Héchel wó'echu," that was the way it was done, when people lived a certain way.

When young girls like me played, we had many dolls. These dolls were made by an older sister or, in my case, by an older female relative since I had no sisters. I had boy and girl dolls, men and women dolls, and even baby dolls. The dolls I preferred were ordinary ones that were not elaborately dressed or decorated.

I had some of those, too, but they were for show and I couldn't play with them as I did the ordinary ones. I also preferred the girl and boy dolls, as well as the men and women ones. I could pretend with these more readily. The baby dolls were not as easy to play with except to pretend that I was a mother with many children. The other dolls I could role-play and do many things with.

I enjoyed "škátapi cík̇ala," playing with dolls and all the small things they had. My dolls had many things, like small cradle boards and even small tipis. The small tipis were made like the real ones. These I played with, imitating the way they used to live. In the old days young girls, like my grandmother Turtle Lung Woman, knew how to make them. They practiced in play how to make real ones. She said the women cut and tanned their own buffalo hides to make their own tipis. They even chose the best lodge poles in the Ȟé Sápa, the Black Hills. They learned in play how to use the things their mothers used. "Otúyachį héchųpišni," they were not merely playing, but learning real skills they would need as women.

Turtle Lung Woman said she learned in play how to take a young sapling and bend it into a hoop and to wrap rawhide thongs on it to make a webbing for a travois. She made small ones and tied them on sticks that she fastened to young dogs to pull the way horses pulled the real ones. Sometimes she would tie it on a willing boy and he would play like he was a horse. She imitated the work of the women back then, the way they moved an entire camp on their travois, she moved her small playthings on hers.

In her "škátapi cík̇ala," or "play with small things," Turtle Lung Woman pretended to cook with miniature pots. She would invite other girls to "wó'icu," mock feasts, and "wiȟpeye," giveaways or gift-giving celebrations. She told me over and over, "Otúyachį héchųpišni," "We didn't just 'play,' we were learning to do all the things women like our mothers, grandmothers, and aunts did." She said they were learning how to give real feasts and giveaways, where generosity was the rule. In this way they learned to value the same things the grown women did.

In time, Turtle Lung Woman was given a small bag with sinew, an awl, and a needle in it, and she learned how to make moccasins. This occurred around puberty, when she was expected to practice skills like tanning and quillwork, even making moccasins during her "išnáthi," when she was in the midst of her menses. Until then, she was free as a young girl to play.

She told me her favorite dolls were made of soft deerskin. The head, arms, and legs were of soft deerskin. A face was usually painted on with black paint with red painted circles where the cheeks were. Sometimes her female dolls wore jewelry like earrings and a choker made of porcupine quills or beadwork. Her female dolls wore old-time belts the way women back then wore them. The female dolls wore buckskin dresses, leggings, and moccasins. The hair used for the dolls was horse hair, neatly braided in the female style or as worn by the men.

The male dolls she played with were dressed in deerskin shirts decorated with simple quillwork or beadwork. The leggings and moccasins worn by the male dolls were also made from soft deerskin. The male dolls had faces drawn on them with black paint. She carried these dolls the way any child carries a favorite toy. Their sizes varied and she kept them all in a special bag, the way she later learned to carry the things she needed to practice her medicine.

Turtle Lung Woman told me a story about a group of young girls who were fond of playing together. There were about five or six of them, each dressed in buckskin clothing like the women, but in ordinary dress, without all the decoration put on special clothing for ceremonial dress. These girls were fond of each other. They were all about the same size and age. They went everywhere together.

One of their favorite games when they weren't playing with their collections of small toys, like dolls and other things, was a game called "hóšišipa." In the game they chanted a phrase, "hóšišipa, hóšišipa, hóšišipa." As they chanted rhythmically, the little girls would stand in a circle and hold their hands out, "hó-ši-ši-pa, hó-ši-ši-pa, hó-ši-ši-pa." They would alternately place one hand over another girl's, and as they did this, they would pinch the loose skin on top of the hand, midway between the wrist and fingers. As they did this, a rule of the game was that the one being pinched could not laugh. The first one to laugh ended the game because they would all laugh, falling in a heap. Throughout the game they were all waiting with bated breaths to see who would laugh first.

One day, while this particular group of girls was out playing, they were told to gather wood for their mothers. It was the women's work to find wood for their fires, and mothers enlisted the help of their daughters when they could. These girls were doing what their mothers had done when they were small. They had the luxury of playing as they gathered the wood. It was while they were trying to reach some dry wood across a small ravine that one of them fell into it. The other girls quickly came to her aid.

When the girl fell, certain body parts were revealed. The others could see that he was not a girl. They had known the "girl" for a long time. In all his mannerisms, he had acted like one of them. He always sat like a young girl with his feet to the side and not cross-legged as a boy. He dressed like one of them, he even wore his hair like a young girl. "Wį́kte hécha," it was said, "he was a boy who acted like a girl." He was not despised for it, he was feared.

Once they saw what he was, the girls abandoned him and ran home. They quickly ran back to camp to tell their mothers. They refused to play with him after that. He was too mysterious. Turtle Lung Woman said that it had to be so, he would be tolerated but left alone. His life would be a lonely one, after that.

She said that a "wį́kte" was one who had a dream that if he lived like a woman he would live a long life. A man among the Lakotas is a warrior and lives with the constant awareness of death. A wį́kte, it was thought, became what he was to avoid death. To a man, it was considered cowardly to "have the heart of a woman." Indeed it was a hard life back then, but, because a wį́kte dressed like a woman and even had the "heart of a woman," he was protected by the men.

The men feared wį́ktes the most. If a man had a relationship with one, it was said that in the spirit world he would not be allowed to see his relatives. He would have to live outside the camp with the murderers and thieves. There he would be tortured by the wį́kte he had the relationship with. This was what the men believed and they were very afraid of them.

The wį́kte would be allowed to live at the edge of the camp circle with others like him who are alone. Those who no longer had families, like widows and orphans. He would be provided for, but he would remain friendless, unless he met others like himself. He would call them "sisters." They were thought to possess certain powers, and if a child, usually a male child, was named by one, he would never face illness. It was said that fathers of beloved sons flirted with them to coerce them into giving their sons names. She said a wįkte never named a girl, that is, never gave her a secret name like he would a young boy.

It seemed unlikely that young girls like Turtle Lung Woman and her friends would attempt the opposite. The boys would not find a girl living among them as a "hokšíla," a young boy. It was because he wanted "maške," meaning "friends" as spoken by the female voice, that the wįkte lived a secret life. He must have longed for them, for the brief time in his life when he enjoyed their friendship when he was thought to be a "wichįcalala," a little girl, the only time in his life when he would have many maške. The wichįcalala, like everyone in the tribe, knew of them and were afraid of them. Turtle Lung Woman did not tell me if she had been a member of that group of young girls. She did not say whether it was she and her friends who rejected the young wįkte.

My Horse Flies Like a Bird

Kholá
mitháš<u>u</u>ke
k<u>i</u>y<u>á</u>y<u>a</u>
í<u>y</u>ake lo

Friend
my horse
he flies like a bird
as he runs

15

Horses of Many Colors

The colors one sees on the plains, "makhóche kị̇," on the earth, are unchanging with the seasons. The hills are the same color except in early spring when we say "pheží šá," "the grass is red." The things that change color are the things that are alive. The things that move upon the land, like the wind on the buffalo grass and the thatháka itself, the great buffalo.

"Líla ehą́ni," a long time ago, in a time long past, Turtle Lung Woman said that certain young men were selected to search the plains for buffalo. She said it was an honor to be chosen. These young men were told to find the buffalo and to help the people locate them. When they returned with news that the plains were black with buffalo, the people grew excited at the prospect of a hunt.

The other animal that filled our lives with meaning was the horse. In time we became as dependent on it as we were the buffalo. In our winter counts, the first horses were found in the 1700s. Back then, it had greater endurance and could travel long distances without water. Perhaps the way it traveled northward from the south, when it escaped from its Spanish owners. It had stamina like the buffalo and the eagle. Some say the first horses came from the west. Some thought that the strange four-legged animal with a long mane was a "šúka tháka," or "big dog," that it was "wakhą́," mysterious.

The Lakota word for horse is "šúkawakhą," "šúka," meaning "dog," and "wakhą́," meaning "sacred." All the tasks that the šúka did for us before 1700, the horse could do. It carried our belongings on a travois. It helped us hunt and ward off the enemy. It was able to do much more than a šúka. It could carry a human being. It was strong enough to do this.

The horse was not just another animal, it caught the imagination of the

Lakota "hokšíla," or "boy." It was his first love. He spent as much time as he could on his pony. He learned how to use a rope made out of buffalo hair to capture his pony. He knew how to break a pony for riding. He learned how to stay on his horse while another boy chased him and tried to pull him off when they played war games. He imitated real life. He learned how to use a knife, bow, and arrow. These things he would need to know how to use well in order to survive as a hunter and warrior. Indeed every hokšíla was encouraged to become a "zuyá wichášà," a warrior, to protect the helpless, the elders, the women and children. His reward would be his reputation as a warrior, to have women sing songs for him about how courageous and cunning he was.

Turtle Lung Woman said there were certain times when a Lakota man painted his horse. He painted his horse right before he rode it into the herd to kill the thathą́ka, the buffalo. He took certain precautions to make sure the horse didn't panic at the strong smell of the thathą́ka. He made it wear a strip of buffalo hide as a halter to get used to the smell. He trained his horse to run with other horses close by so that in the actual hunt he could ride next to the great animal and shoot an arrow into its heart. When an arrow hits close to the heart, the thathą́ka stops and stands still or lies down, making it easier for the hunter to finish the kill.

Turtle Lung Woman said when my grandfather Ité Sįyą́khiya painted himself as a zuyá wicháša with clay, he painted his horse with the same clay. He painted his šų́kawakhą to invoke its sacredness, just as he painted himself. He revered it, particularly the one he rode into battle or into a herd of buffalo. He painted it to signify that it is a sacred animal, a messenger of Wakį́yą, the thunder being. It was believed then that the horse came from the west, where the dreaded thunder being dwells. The power of Wakį́yą resided in it. It did the bidding of that terrible being. It came to kill, the way the thunder being has the power to destroy. So, too, the horse gives man the ability to slaughter the great thathą́ka for the good of all. In times of war, it allowed him to count coup, then slay his enemy.

Lakota men were vigilant when it came to enemy raids and intrusion into our hunting territory, "Lakhóta ú ektá," where our people dwelled. Indeed, this territory extended from North Dakota to Kansas, Colorado, and into Minnesota. It was a vast area well-guarded by the Lakota men. They would go to war over it, or sometimes go to war for more horses. Whatever the reason, when they were done with war, the men washed themselves and their horses, "ic'íkpakhįta," wiping away the paint, to resume their lives as before.

The paints the men used were prepared by women like my grandmother Turtle Lung Woman. On the plains she would dig a small hole to make fire to heat stones for cooking. Turtle Lung Woman said a special hole was dug when the women wanted to help the men prepare the paint they used to paint themselves and their horses. The paints they used came from a powder made from an ocher material that was mixed with buffalo fat to produce yellow paint. When the same substance was baked in a hole dug in the ground, the heat turned it red.

The women made a special fire in the hole to heat it. They dug a small deep hole and carefully built a fire in it. While it burned they took the powdery ocher material, mixed it with water, and formed it into a ball. When the fire burned itself out, the women used antlers from a deer to rake the hot coals out. They placed the ball of ocher upon the warm earth and covered it with the coals. They built another fire on top of it. The heat changed the color of the ocher to red. The red ball of ocher was cooled and pounded into a powder. It was kept in a small bag and mixed with buffalo fat when it was needed to produce red paint.

There were other paints made with clay or earthen materials that were found only in certain places. There is a place in Minnesota where the earth is "thó," blue. This blue earth was used the same way, it was mixed with buffalo fat to produce blue paint. There is "makhá ská," or "white earth," that is found on the plains, just as there is "makhá ǧí," or "brown earth." These are used to make paint as well. Sometimes these colors are made with plant dyes but those colors were unreliable. The genuine colors were red, yellow, white, and black, made from the earth. These colors never fade. They are our sacred colors.

I remember one family, the Young Dogs, who had a hokšíla who made a whole village of miniature tipis. This boy made the whole village, "mayá aglágla," along the ravine where he played. He had horses made from the dried hooves of buffalo. His mother had collected and dried the hooves of buffalo for him. His father painted horses of many colors on one side of the hoof. He painted "šügléška," spotted horses, "šügmákhicima," young horses, and even "šükchí-cala," young colts. The hokšíla played with them as if they were real. They reared up on their hind legs and filled the village with neighing and galloping noises. He made the "šükawakhą kįyą" like "zįtkála," he made the horses fly like birds as they raced here and there. You could almost see their nostrils flaring the way the horses looked when they exerted themselves in the hunt or battle in the old days.

When I think about that time, as I watched the boy playing along the ravine, I hear the boy's father singing, "Kholá, mithášüké kįyáyą íyąke lo": "Friend, my horse flies like a bird as he runs." I imagine that was what he sang as he painted the buffalo hooves.

Little Girl's Chant

Hóšišipa
Hóšišipa
Hóšišipa
Hóši

Whispers

I started at the school they called Number Sixteen when I was six years old. I went to what was called primary school at the day school operated by the federal government. It was not a boarding school, so all of the children came in the morning and went home in the late afternoon.

What I remember was "hél iȟpé mayápi," they took me and left me there at that place. I did not go home with my mother and father as I had done when we took my older brothers there. I did not want to stay, but I had no choice. It was a law, we had to attend school, our parents were told. A truant officer rode out to everyone's house on horseback to enforce the law. If a school-age child didn't go to school, the truant officer would come and pick them up and take them on horseback to Number Sixteen.

It was one building, with one classroom and a kitchen. It looked like a house. It was not a large structure. There was a separate building next to it where the teacher and his wife lived. An outhouse stood next to the school. This was similar to the ones placed near each of our homes in our small community.

Outside the building where the classes were held stood a flagpole, and a "wíyokhihe," a flag, an American one, hung from it. It was hung each day before the school day began and taken down when the day ended. We learned to say the Pledge of Allegiance every morning to begin the school day. I can still remember it, the way we held our right hands over our hearts and recited it.

I went there every day. In the late afternoon they would come for me. I looked forward to that time when I could go home and be with my parents, Mom-mah and Pah-pah. It seemed like a long day and I was always glad to be home. Again, in the morning they would bring me there and leave me.

So I went every day, as did a lot of other children. "Eš, táku wó'uspe'ukhiyapi kį hé," but what they taught us was this, we could not speak Lakota, our native language. "Wašícu ųkhíya," they made us speak English. It was the only language allowed at the school.

We as children felt repressed by this new language. How odd it felt to try to speak English. We fell silent in the presence of our teacher at the school. What could we say in this new language that would communicate how we felt? We could not speak it well enough to understand each other, and secretly we laughed at ourselves, at our struggle to say something, anything, in this foreign tongue.

The language I heard in my mother's womb was Lakota. It was not this awkward one that felt clumsy on my tongue. I tripped over it many times. I knew then I would never understand or speak it the way they wanted me to. How stifled I felt, for even then I was outspoken and knew my place in my world.

In my family, I was Wíyą Išnála, Lone Woman, the only "wichícala," young girl, in a family of five boys, and I was special. My parents encouraged me to feel this way. I was allowed to speak my mind, to express myself, even at a young age. My brothers observed it, seeing how my parents encouraged it, and they too indulged me. Now I could not speak the language I knew best, to say what I wanted to, whenever I wanted. I could not express how I felt about this new place, called "owáyawa," school. I knew how "zįtkála," the bird, or "khąǧí", the crow, felt when they split its tongue and made it speak.

The word "owáyawa" meant "a place where one learns to read." It is the name we used to signify a place the wašícu called "school." "Wa'ųspe'ic'iya," we were told, "Teach yourself" the white man's words. Indeed, it appeared that we were teaching ourselves. Our parents, who traditionally had that role, were no longer with us throughout the day. We had to adjust to this new way, where we sat alone in the classroom and tried our best to learn what the teacher said we should know.

When we weren't seen, or heard, we spoke Lakota. In secret we whispered to each other. "Nahmáhma Lakhótiya woglákapi," we children spoke it in hushed tones. The teacher did not always see us so we whispered in Lakota as we played. How could we play together in English, a language we did not know how to speak? How could we play the old games in this new language? When the teacher caught us, he punished us by putting us indoors. We had to sit at our desks through recess and miss one of the only chances to play with our friends.

There were two teachers, Mr. Clapper and Mrs. Clapper, his wife. They worked together. She taught primary school and he taught the older kids. There must have been thirty or forty of us. His wife was also a cook. She cooked our meals and taught us girls how to sew. What I remember about Mr. Clapper was how big his hands were and how large he was. When I was six years old, I was afraid of him. He seemed like a very large person, especially to a small child like me when I first started at that school.

When school began in the autumn, the government gave us clothing. The girls they gave dress material. Mrs. Clapper taught us how to use the sewing machine. We had all of our lessons in the morning. In the afternoon Mrs. Clapper taught us other skills. She showed us how to cut the material and make our own dresses. Once we learned how to cut patterns for dresses, we took the material and cut it at home. She would help us sew the patterns at school, the next day. In this way, we learned how to make our own dresses. The government issued us stockings and shoes. The boys received clothing as well. They received pants, shirts, suspenders, and socks. They received a pair of sturdy shoes to wear during the school year. Whatever we were given at the beginning of the school year had to last through the whole year.

I remember how the teacher liked celebrations, and every school holiday he would give a feast and invite all the parents. They came and enjoyed feasting with Mr. Clapper and his wife. He especially loved Christmas, and it was then that he gave the largest feast. We children would do a special Christmas program for our parents.

Our parents respected him. They liked him, and he, in turn, seemed to enjoy his role there. He was a leader, they looked up to him because he looked after the children. "Wa'úspe'ukhiyapi," he and his wife taught us. They taught us many things that I still remember.

We children ate lunch at the school. We called "lunch" "dinner," and when it was dinnertime we ate at our desks. "Éna desk uyákapi kį hená šna, eyá wakšíca ahí'ukiglepi," they served us our lunch while we remained seated at our desks. The teacher's wife cooked these meals for us and set out bowls for each of us at our desks. Mr. Clapper and his wife handed out generous portions for each of us, portions of bread, molasses, beans, and water. I dipped my bread in the thick molasses and ate it quickly. I loved sweets even then.

When lunch was over, we washed our own "wakšíca," bowl, and our own cup and utensils, and put them away. The day continued, "akhé wa'úyawapi," again we read and learned the things they thought we should know. The way our parents used to teach us at home. We now had to learn this new way. I was glad for the opportunity to return "wathí ektá," to my home, at the end of the day. There, the old way of learning continued, in a different way.

The Sunrise

Wí hináphe	The sun rises
waláka nuwé	may you behold
wí hináphe	the sun rises
waláka nuwé lo	may you behold
wí hináphe	the sun rises
waláka nuwé lo	may you behold
wí hináphe	the sun rises
waláka nuwé	may you behold
o he	so it is

17

The Grasses They Grew – Part 1

I did not go to school for the full year. My school year began in December, right before Christmas, and continued through the end of the school year in June. I remember in the mid-1920s how it was in my family. In early June, my father and other families began preparing to leave the reservation to find work in the farm fields in Nebraska. When we left in June we did not return until early December.

There was no other income on the reservation for men like Pah-pah. He could not expect money from any other source. So we packed a large canvas tent, tent poles, and other necessities and went into Nebraska to find work in the fields to earn money to live on. We lived in Nebraska for those seven months. We made trips home to the reservation for brief visits, but we had to travel all summer to different jobs in the fields.

In Nebraska we set up camp at the northern edge of town at Tháȟca Wak-pála, Deer Creek. At the outskirts of town, there was a barn, stable, and large camp ground. We put up our horses at the barn and stable. We pitched our tent at the camp ground. There, other families like us were camped. They came to find work for the summer, too. Some of the Lakota people lived all year in the camp ground. We only stayed until the winter came and then we went home. We made occasional trips home during the summer, but we lived primarily on the go, traveling from job to job.

In the month of June, the month we call Thípsila Itkáȟca Wí, The Moon When the Wild Turnips Ripen, we started out toward Nebraska. There in the fields the men like Thatȟáka Náží would start work by weeding or tending the growing crops the farmers planted, like potato plants. In July, during the month we call Chaphása Wí, The Moon of Red Chokecherries, the men would go into the wheat and oat fields.

Thatháka Nážį and the other men learned to cultivate the wheat and oats according to the farmers' instructions. By the time we arrived in June, the farmers had already planted the wheat in a north-south orientation for wind protection or diagonally for the rain. The oats they planted in fields where they had rotated different crops like corn or clover. They grew many crops like wheat, oats, corn, potatoes, and sugar beets even in dry areas, with irrigation. The water for their irrigation ditches came from the river we called Phakéska Wakpá, or Shell Creek. The wašícu called it the Platte River.

The summer months fell into one growing season or another for the various crops. We followed each season, each one required different work from the men like Thatháka Nážį. In those days the farmers relied on them during the growing season and at harvest time. The area near the Platte River had richer soil and a variety of crops; there the men found more work in the fields.

The rich soil along the Platte River is nothing like that on the reservation. We grew small gardens back home on the reservation near Porcupine Creek. Our gardens were meager compared to these large farms that produced great harvests, farms that required the work of several Indian families in the summer and autumn months.

At home we grew "wagméza," corn, "wagmú," pumpkins, "wagmú blú," squash, "wagmúšpašni," watermelon, "thípsila skaská," white turnips, "thípsila šašá," radishes, and "thípsila zizí," carrots, on medium-sized plots. These came from seeds that the government gave to us and taught us how to plant.

One of the few roots that we ate grew wild on the plains. It is "thípsila," a wild turnip that we harvest in June. It is the only root we dig from the earth to eat for nourishment. There were other roots we ate for medicine. Thípsila is the only root similar to the seeds that we were given to grow and harvest, so we called every root "thípsila," including turnips, radishes, and carrots. A carrot is called "thípsila zizí," referring to the color of the root, "zizí" meaning "yellow." We also called squash and plants like squash that grew from a blossom "wagmú."

These words did not exist until we were put on reservations and given seeds to grow. We were not farmers as Lakota people, but we are survivors and we adapted. We learned to grow things in the ground in order to live, especially after the buffalo disappeared.

Many of the families on the reservation had gardens. "Blokétu ópta," through the summer, "wóžupi," a garden was planted and tended at home for our family. Those that remained behind on the reservation cared for them, while the rest of us traveled in search of work. Turtle Lung Woman, my grandmother, watched our garden. She loved the harvest, when she could cook the squash and sprinkle sugar on it. She ate the soft mushy inside, enjoying the sweet strong taste of squash or pumpkin. I did not like it as much as the adults did. I like the "wagmúšpašni," the watermelon.

Thathą́ka Ną́žį built a long root cellar and stored our harvest from the garden in it. The root cellar is a structure built by digging into the ground where earthen shelves serve as storage areas for the pumpkins, squash, and even the watermelons that we stored on straw. We knew that during a long winter nothing would be wasted. "Hená áta yuwíya ékignakapi," they set things aside in readiness. The people prepared all summer for the long winter months when food was hard to come by.

All the crops Thathą́ka Ną́žį and the men harvested for the farmers in Nebraska, the wašícu brought from Europe, the place we call Mni'ówąca, or "across the ocean." Oats, wheat, and other grasses cultivated by the farmers in Nebraska came from there. These plants were new to us and to the land. When our people roamed the Nebraska plains, it was grazing land for the buffalo. The wašícu brought seeds, built houses out of sod dug from the earth, planted their seeds, and stayed.

The Lakota men hoed the rows of potato, wheat, corn, and oat plants. They separated the crop from the weeds and tended them. "Yu'óslata églepi," they made it so the plants stood straight and tall. They worked hard to make sure each plant was free from weeds and disease. They worked in the potato fields, "okó, hená," through the planted rows. This required a lot of hand labor and hard work in the dry heat of the Nebraska sun. That was what my father and the other Lakota men did in June and July.

All summer and autumn we went where there were jobs. We moved from one work site to another, from farmhouse to farmhouse. "Héchel ųkómanipi," that was the way we lived for seven months out of every year. I remember one farm that we lived at for a short while. When you first cross the state line into Nebraska, going south from the reservation, the farm sits at the end of a long lane hidden by a long row of cottonwood trees. The farmer planted these to provide wind protection on the flat plains and to keep snow from drifting over the lane in the winter.

I remember one summer when my father worked there. We camped at a site on the farm. One day I was ill and the farmer's wife said she would take me into town. The woman had red hair and the people called her Phešá, meaning "red top," like the comb of the rooster. She had a Model T Ford and said she would drive us into town. Thatháka Nážį, Mom-mah, and I climbed into the Model T with her. She took us into town, and after I saw the doctor she invited us to have lunch with her. She brought out a picnic basket, and we sat under a tree to eat. Thatháka Nážį looked in disdain at the boiled eggs and cheese sandwiches she brought out. He did not like the smell of the food. He took it but later threw it away. My mother said he stole away and bought something more appropriate to eat.

We even traveled south into Nebraska across the Niobrara River. "Wakpá akhó-tąhą," we worked beyond the river in the hay fields. They summoned us to work in the fields and we went. "Pheží églepi cha, hená wicháša kį wa'ókiyapi," the men worked harvesting hay. The farmers grew alfalfa, clover, oats, or other grasses for hay. The men like Thatháka Nážį had to help harvest it at the right time or it wouldn't be good for fodder. It was hard work, but the men went into the fields every year. It was after Thatháka Nážį had been haying in August that Mom-mah gave birth to me in a camp ground in Nebraska.

144

The best grass for hay in the dry land of Nebraska is the buffalo grass. It dries without being cut and loses very little of its food value. In the old days, our horses ate it and lived well on it. Now, the farmers there rely on the seeds from the grasses they brought from across the ocean. Some of these grasses, like clover, if cut too late, would cause stomach ailments and bowel problems in horses, and even death. We didn't have to cut grass and store it for our horses. We let them graze naturally on the wild grass just as the buffalo had for centuries.

The men did thrashing in the wheat and oat fields. When it came time to thrash, the work required them to labor by hand. In those days the farmers relied on hand labor. This was before the combines or combine-harvesters. When it was thrashing time, Thatháka Náži and the other Lakota men worked long hours. They ate lunch in the fields. The foreman would bring it for them to save time. Mom-mah sent me into the fields to bring Pah-pah sugared coffee in a jar. We stayed nearby and watched Pah-pah and the other Lakota men work.

"Ųkó'ųyąpi," we lived that way all summer. "Blokétu áta héchel okó manípi," all summer long we traveled that way, from job site to job site, from field to field. "Hóyena, ecé šna ptąyétu chą," so it went, until autumn. Then it was time to harvest the potatoes. "Blopáhipi wą hiyú," potato picking time came quickly upon us.

When it was time to harvest the potatoes, everyone worked, including the women. I was younger then, so I could not work in the fields, but Mom-mah did. My brother's wives worked as well. So, I watched the children. I was the youngest in my family, but I had nephews and nieces that were five years or more my junior, and I watched them. "Hokší awáblake," I watched the children for the women in my family who were working in the fields.

I also had the important job of cooking. I made coffee, tea, bread, and soup for everyone in my family. I was quick with my hands and I knew how to make good bread. I mixed flour, baking powder, water, and melted lard in a bowl and kneaded it to make flat skillet bread. I stacked the bread on a plate and everyone pulled a smaller piece from it to eat. I knew how to peel and slice potatoes and fry them in a skillet for lunch. I could make soup with potatoes, turnips, and boiling meat for an evening meal.

When everyone came home in the late afternoon, our camp smelled of bread cooking in a skillet and coffee over an open fire. I learned how to make both coffee and tea in pots over the open fire. Mom-mah liked tea and Pah-pah drank strong coffee. I grew up liking hot sugared tea. I never drank coffee and did not even bother to taste the black brew that my Pah-pah and the others called "wakhályapi," or "heated it is."

On those summer evenings when everyone came back to the camp after working all day in the potato fields, the children ran playing. I no longer had to watch them. The men and women washed their dusty faces in the metal wash basins. The women shook out aprons that they had hung by their tent doors. They wrapped their aprons around themselves as easily as they had worn the potato picking belts in the potato fields. The smell of food was in the air and everyone prepared to sit down for supper. The men visited and counted the days before payday.

I looked forward to Saturdays, when no one worked and we went into town to shop. My brothers, whose children I watched, would pay me by buying me something. It wasn't just my brothers, but everyone whom I cooked for, who would pool their money and buy me a jacket or something I needed for winter. I worked all summer this way, earning things I needed.

In September and October, when potato picking ended, the men and women worked in the corn fields, helping the farmers harvest the crop. I would again resume my jobs as cook and babysitter. "Ho hé akhé héchupi," again they labored in the fields. We moved our tents, "echékce uthípi," from place to place. "Hená waší echúya ománipi," we worked from farm to farm, living in our tents.

My grandmother Turtle Lung Woman was born in 1851, three years before the government passed an act creating the territory of Nebraska. Before that it had been called Indian Territory. When my grandmother was sixteen years old, Nebraska became a state.

Turtle Lung Woman knew the old roads and in which direction lived our enemies and our allies. In the old days, the Phaláni, the Pawnees, our enemies, lived in what is now southwest Nebraska. The Oyáte Yámni, meaning "three tribes," referred to the Poncas along with the Omahas and Otos, who lived along the Missouri River. We lived in what is now western Nebraska near our allies the Šahíyela, the Cheyennes, and Maȟpíya Thó, or "blue clouds," the Arapahos.

The land that had been home to all of us was given away by the federal government, first as 160-acre sections per settler, then further into 640 acres for one settler to homestead. By 1904, when Turtle Lung Woman was fifty-three years old, the land was no longer wide-open space. The appearance of more and more farms meant that fences were coming closer and closer together, and barbed wire fences crisscrossed the land. Turtle Lung Woman decided then that she did not want to travel into Nebraska.

From Everywhere They Come

Tókhiyatą k'eyá	From somewhere
a'ú we	they come
kįyą́	flying
wazíyatą	from the north
thatúye	the wind blows
makhátą	to earth
icášna	rattling
kįyą́	flying
a'ú we	they come
a'ú we	they come
tókhiyatą k'eyá	from everywhere
a'ú we	they come

18

The Grasses They Grew – Part 2

My father and mother went into Nebraska in those days so that they could buy food to live through the long winters. When I was younger, there was no other way to survive. They did this to live. They worked and saved their pay. On Saturday they bought food in large quantities. They shopped at a store in Tháȟča Wakpála owned by a man named Joe. "Lé Lakhóta óp tȟayá ú," he got along well with the Lakota people. His store was an important place for everyone.

I don't remember anyone calling him anything but "Joe." He treated us well, and we shopped in his store every Saturday. He would allow people to put things on layaway. They would pay him each payday. Sometimes he would just store items that we bought and paid for until we could get them home to the reservation. On one side of his store he had a storeroom he allowed us to use. "Christmas wa'ícu kí táku icú kį hená hél ékignakapi," whatever they purchased for Christmas they kept there.

"Ho héchel ųkáya na, ųkáya na," that was how it went while we lived there. Those summer, autumn, and early-winter months were spent in Nebraska. In December when it became too cold to live in a tent, we started for home. We left Nebraska and headed north into South Dakota. We went by automobile, in a Model T Ford that my oldest brother owned. We also relied on our wagon pulled by two horses, but the Model T was faster and a good way to get us home. The cold winds of early December were too harsh for the younger children.

They loaded us into the Model T Ford of Zįtkála Ská, White Bird, my oldest brother, and we drove home. White Bird's Model T had wheels smaller than our wagon. It had whitewall tires and looked fancy. We called it and other automobiles "iyéchįkįyąka," meaning "it runs on its own." It seemed large to me, as a child. It had a step that I had to step high onto, a door that was hard for me to open, and windows that seemed high and hard to look out of. I liked the feel of the seat as we bounced along on our way home to the reservation.

We children came home first. Ụcí, my grandmother Turtle Lung Woman, who remained behind on the reservation, was always glad to see us. She would notify our other relatives who also stayed behind and by the late afternoon on the next day when the grownups returned, all of our relatives would come to welcome them home. That was the way it was back then, whenever anyone came back from Nebraska it was a big event. Our relatives came for news, but mostly to share in our good fortune. When we all came together we feasted.

When they came back the next day, the grownups arrived in the late afternoon, sometimes early evening. A long time ago it took a day to travel by wagon from Tháľica Wakpála in Nebraska. In those days everything required more time and people moved slowly and deliberately. They took their time and did everything carefully and well. "Áta chạpágmiyạpi ogná šna wa'áglipi," they brought a load home on their wagon to help us survive the winter.

In the late summer and early autumn when we made visits home to the reservation, Pah-pah and my brothers gathered firewood. "Óp chạ tokšú," he carted wood home with them. Sometimes my father and mother would climb into their wagon and leave in the morning, returning home in the late afternoon with a wagon full of wood. My father sat in the driver's seat on the left side facing the horses; my mother sat in the passenger seat, wrapped in her blanket. They were always on the move, always preparing for some future event. When they began gathering wood, it was in earnest. The winters in South Dakota were long and severe.

My father was always thinking ahead. He brought logs home for firewood. He had a purification lodge and he brought home enough wood for that as well. The things he would need for the long winter, he carefully gathered. Pah-pah and my brothers made sure we had enough wood. We needed it to heat our large log house. Turtle Lung Woman, my grandmother, had a smaller log house and she needed firewood too. When I look around me, now, at the sparse trees along the ridge here on the reservation, I wonder where they found all the wood that they did.

Even when we were traveling in Nebraska, "aglí waỵákapi," Pah-pah and Mommah came home to the reservation to check on things. They would return to see if everything was alright at home. When they did, "wa'ágli kpeyápi," they would bring home sacks of flour, sugar, or potatoes or other food they bought. They were always concerned with whether they had enough food for the long winter.

In December, the month we call Thahécapšu Wí, The Moon in Which the Deer Shed Their Horns, or sometimes Waníchoka Wí, meaning "midwinter," we came back to the reservation. The cold winter, the lack of work, and the fact that Christmas was close brought us home. When we came back my parents brought everything, including the tent, tent poles, fire grates used for cooking, and all of our personal belongings. "Táku iyúha gloglípi," they brought back all the things they carried from camp to camp in Nebraska.

My mother and father, Mom-mah and Pah-pah, began preparing for Christmas as soon as we arrived home. It was an event they looked forward to. A chance to see all of their relatives, friends, and people in the community. They looked forward to the feasts. They celebrated the fact we were home. They looked upon Christmas as a time of goodwill, feasting, and giving to others. It seemed to be a perfect Lakota celebration with all the good food and generosity exhibited toward all.

"Christmas hená iyé tháwapi," Christmas belonged to Mom-mah and Pah-pah. It was theirs. "Iyé waká hená tháwapi," it belonged to the elders. Christmas was their time. They took full responsibility for it. It was no small task. In those days, everyone had to be self-sufficient, we knew nothing of charity.

Pah-pah and Mom-mah were members of the Episcopal Church. They helped celebrate Christmas at the church. They prepared a great Christmas feast and everyone came. They bought apples and oranges in boxes for the children. They put together small paper sacks of peanuts, walnuts, and filberts mixed with Christmas candy, usually peppermint, for the children.

I looked forward to Christmas as a young child. Sometimes uçí Turtle Lung Woman would give me her bag of peanuts and candy. I would hide them from my brothers and enjoyed them long after Christmas. I received one gift on Christmas Eve. It was given to me by Wazíya, or Santa Claus, who came to see the children at the Christmas Eve service at the Episcopal church. He gave us our gifts then. In the old days, the word "wazíya" meant all the character-istics of the power of the north wind, Wazíyata. The cold north wind and its power to take life. The mysterious north whose powers were sacred. It was the name we gave to the character introduced to us, whom they said came from the north. When the service was over, all the men shook hands and bid "Merry Christmas" to each other in English. It sounded like "Mary Krismus," to me, as a child, I liked the sound of it, it meant good things.

So it went, after Christmas, on New Year's Eve, there was a powwow or dance celebration. Again, Mom-mah and Pah-pah were involved. They put on a din-ner or feast at the powwow. They were always busy in our community. Pah-pah was an Omaha dancer and he would dance at the powwow. His "phéša," or head ornament, bouncing in rhythm to the drums at the New Year's Eve powwow.

In January, the month we call Wi'óchokạyạ Wí, The Midwinter Moon, or sometimes we called it Wi'óthehika Wí, or The Moon When Hardships Are Many, the weather is unpredictable. The winter snow could turn without warn-ing into a blizzard and everyone stayed near home, no one traveled much, especially into Nebraska. It was a time to sit at home and take care of the things that one wasn't able to do during the busy year. A time to sew, repair harnesses, or to visit with relatives. It was a time I returned to school full-time. I began my year in December and stayed through June. That was why, "owáya kị hé," this thing they called schooling, I did not have a lot of. I only went a portion of the year. "Míyecuňci lílaňci wabláwašni," myself, I did not have as much schooling as some.

"Iyókogna ób šnaománwani, iyúha tókhel ománipi héchel omáwani," in between, from June through early December, I traveled with my family. When we came home to the reservation, "aglí na akhé hetá wayápi," from that time forward I went to school again. I learned again how to read and write. I was forbidden again to speak my native language.

I know my family could have taken me and left me at the government boarding school or the Catholic boarding school in Pine Ridge while they traveled into Nebraska to find work. I am thankful they didn't. If they had, I would have forgotten as a young child how to speak this language that I hold close to my heart. I would have forgotten these things that I remember, what my grandmother Turtle Lung Woman told me to remember, in Lakota. I did not forget because I went with them. There in Nebraska, they spoke it, while they worked in the fields. I was there and I remember.

Song of the Buffalo Calf Woman

Niyá thạ'íyạ	With visible breath
mawáni ye	I am walking
oyáte lé	this nation
imáwani	I walk toward
na	and
hóthạ'íyạ	my voice is heard
mawáni ye	I am walking
niyá thạ'íyạ	with visible breath
mawáni ye	I am walking
walúta lé	this sacred red object
imáwani ye	for it, I walk

19

Canvas Moccasins

When I was a young girl, what I noticed about the women of my mother's generation was the long dresses they wore. These dresses extended down to their ankles. Their dresses had long sleeves and high collars that came up to the neck as well. They covered every part of themselves. That was how I saw them dress, "ináwaye kį hé," that mother of mine, too.

The way they dressed reflected the way they lived, their quiet manner. We Lakota women were sometimes thought to be prudish. It may have been so, "tuwéni lená makhúg lená etą́hą ų́šni," no one wore clothing showing the neck or legs. They were too modest. My mother felt the same way. "Hená awą́gla-kapi," they "watched themselves," they selected their clothing styles carefully, to make sure that they reflected the old way.

My grandmothers conducted themselves in a similar manner. My father's mother, Kheglézela Chağúwį, Turtle Lung Woman, lived with us for many years, and I watched how she behaved. She acted the way my mother and maternal grandmother did, her demeanor was exactly the same.

What I noticed about them was they wore moccasins made of canvas. Kheglézela Chağúwį wore canvas moccasins that had leather trimmings, the heel and toe were leather. These shoes were made with thick cowhide soles. They were what we called "everyday" shoes and were not usually worn in public. She wore stockings and "hųská," or leggings, that were made of red and blue felt.

My mother wore canvas moccasins, too. When she was going somewhere my mother put on her leather beaded moccasins. When my mother went out, "ąpétu wąží hé tókhiya yį́kta hą́tą," that is, on any day she decided to go somewhere, she dressed appropriately. Growing up, I noticed that it was not only in the way she dressed but also her mannerisms that reflected who she was.

I watched the way my mother behaved when she went to visit her relatives. She had one sister and one brother. She always saw them gladly, "iyúškįya," we say, "with a good heart." In turn, her sister, Ella, and her brother, Frank, were always glad to see her. It seemed to me, as a child, that they lived the old way, "iyúškįya," with goodwill toward others. They appreciated and respected each other as relatives.

My mother and my father both treated all their relatives this way. In turn, their relatives on either side responded the same way. My father had only one brother. My grandfather had other wives, as was customary back then. So, my father had not only his brother, Sįté, Tail, but he had a half-brother, Hupú Chąsákala, or Swallow, that he was close to. Swallow was not Turtle Lung Woman's son. He was a different woman's son.

At the age of twelve, "wachį́waksape," that is, I became fully aware. It was then that I observed everything around me with keen eyes. I saw the women and the way they were. The way they dressed, what they did privately and publicly, and I liked what I saw. I tried to imitate them, the women in my life, particularly the things my mother and grandmother Turtle Lung Woman did. I stayed close to them and learned from them everything I could about how I should conduct myself.

When they went somewhere, in the winter, the women in my family always wore sweaters with a blanket covering both shoulders. They wrapped themselves that way, in beautiful blankets. These blankets were gifts from the government, back then, good things like that were given away. In the summer and warmer months they would carry a shawl or lighter blanket.

In the old days they would take the skin of a young female buffalo and use it for a robe. In those days, all women had robes, beautiful ones that they decorated themselves. The men and children wore them, too, out of necessity, in the cold winter months. The men wore robes, too, sometimes with their right shoulder uncovered. The women and children always wore them with both shoulders fully covered. It was the same way they wore the blankets.

In the winter the hair is left on the buffalo hide, and in the summer it is scraped off to make it lighter. The outer side is always painted or decorated with quills. The younger unmarried women decorated theirs differently from the married or older women. It was said that one could glance at a woman standing with a robe over both shoulders and know immediately if she was single or married.

The women "glastó na anúkisupi," they combed their hair and wore two braids on each side. If the woman wore her braids to the back, it meant that she was single and available. If she wore her braids to the front, it indicated that she was married and unavailable.

The women never cut their hair unless it was for a specific reason, as in the death of a loved one. The hair was always worn long and braided. They cared for it meticulously. The word "phehį" signified "hair," "phé" meaning "the top of the head" and "hį" meaning "fur, down, or hair." It was thought that one's phehį contained one's spirit, and it was treated with reverence, as you would any part of the body of a person. There was a special ceremony for hair cutting and it was always observed. When it was cut from a person's head, it retained the spirit of that person and it had to be treated carefully.

In all their ways "ahóchįphapi," they cared for themselves well. "Ahókipha" or "ahópha," these are important words to us. "Ahókipha" means "to value," and "ahópha" means "to care for one's own." That was the way these women were, my mother and paternal grandmother. They cared about themselves and the people around them. They valued themselves, their children, and their homes. My mother's behavior was always respectful. The things she did I remember well.

My mother danced, and her regalia included a "thahá chuwígnaka," a dress made of elk skin. It was made from two such skins. The upper half was decorated with elk's teeth, about six rows of them, positioned an inch apart. There would be, at the top row, about twelve of the oval-shaped teeth, each measuring an inch or so. She would wear jewelry, earrings of dentalium shells, and several necklaces made of large beads the size of seeds. She wore one strand like a string of pearls around her neck, the other strands much longer and looping in several strands down to her belt. She was a handsome woman.

She wore a "šinágluhapi," a shawl, as in the old days, when she would have worn a buffalo robe over her shoulders. She wore beaded moccasins and "hųská," or "leggings." She, like the other women, danced in one spot. "Tóhạni wíyạ kịhą́ íyạgyạkakišni na'íš glakíyạ iyápišni," that is, the women did not run around or parade themselves in any way. I will say, "Iglú'onihạpi," "they were respectful" in all their movements when they danced.

That was the way she was in everything she did. "Wó'echụ waštéšte," her ways were good to observe. The way she sewed and "wakšú," beaded. The way she cooked and cleaned. Whatever she did, always, it was for the purpose of having the best household. That was what she wanted. "Thiwáhe yuhá chị́," we say, "she wanted a good home."

I followed close behind my mother, that was the way I learned. "Ųšákpepi eš," there were six of us. She treated us all the same. "Iyúha eyá kịhą́ chạté'ųki-yuzapi," that is, she seemed to love us equally. I was one of six children, five boys and one girl. I stayed near her, it was always that way, it seemed. I was her responsibility in a good way. "Wahéhạ, iná mitháwa o'ų́ye tháwa kị hé, wạbláke," I observed her ways with clear eyes. The boys were my father's responsibility. "Atéwaye kị hé," my father taught them what they needed to know.

My mother did not go to school, but she could read and write. She could read and write in Lakota. My father did as well. She could sign her name in English. She was literate in English. "Ináwaye kị hé wíyạ wašté hécha, ephị́kte. Wíyạ wašté cha ináwaye," my mother was good. I do not hesitate to say so. My mother was a good woman. "O'ų́ye tháwapi hé ithą́ imácaǧe," her way, as well as that of my grandmother, their way of life was all I knew, it was what I saw growing up. "Ináwaye kị héchel ụ́ na echél iyá," it was the way my mother lived until one day she left me. She went without me to that place where all of our relatives go when they die. As I speak of her, "iyómakišice eš," I grow sad, but I will continue.

Song of the Shuffling-Feet Dance

Wąchíyąka	I want to see you
wachį́ na	that is what
ecíyatąhą	I desire
wa'ú	on your side
	I will come

20

My Father Was a Dancing Man

My father, Thatȟáka Nážį, "wachí wicháša hécha," he was a dancing man. As long as I remember, he danced the Omáha Dance, which the Lakotas learned from the Omaha people. This dance had great significance for the person performing, like many things among the Lakotas. This was because no one did anything on a whim, all things were done for a reason. In the olden times, this dance was done by men who had a dream.

In the past when they danced, they dressed appropriately according to the dance they intended to do. They prepared themselves both physically and mentally for these dances. "Ho," it was the way I saw it done, a long time ago, the way these things were done.

There were the sacred dances, the "wichóȟ'ą," traditions, that were done. These included the Wichákicilową, or "Singing for Others"; the Wacháśthųpi, or the "Naming Songs"; the Chéȟ'ohomni Wachípi, or the "Circle the Kettle Dance." In many of these dances my father "itȟácha," or "was in charge." We, in his family, supported my father by sitting nearby as spectators, "wawág ųyákapi." He was a "wachí wicháša," a dancing man, and he danced in the center for all to see.

My father's special dance was the Omáha Wachípi, or Grass Dance. We called it "pheží mignáka," or "grass tucked under the belt," the way the men used to tuck scalps from the enemy tribes under their belts. His regalia consisted of a long red loin cloth. He was stripped bare of clothing otherwise, except for a pair of beaded moccasins. He wore a hair ornament made of porcupine hair called a "roach." It resembled a crown of light brown hair bristling over his head, down the back of his neck, to his upper back. On top of the porcupine roach he affixed two eagle feathers on a swivel-like attachment that allowed the feathers to move easily when he danced.

He wore a bone necklace covering his entire chest. It was a rectangular piece of jewelry made with two rows of long ivory pieces resembling long bones, each about five inches long. The entire piece measured a foot across and two feet in length, covering a man's chest. It looked plain, its ivory color light against his reddish-brown skin. It extended from below the neckline, where a choker would be worn, down to just below the waist.

He wore a pair of leather strips, about two and a half feet long, down the outer sides of his legs, down to his knees. Strung on the leather in intervals hung bells measuring about an inch wide. Sometimes these leather strips were longer for other men, hanging down almost to their feet, where a string of bells circled each ankle of the dancer. My father also wore two quill arm bands decorated in red and black with geometric designs.

The most ornate piece of regalia he wore was the long feather bustle tied around his waist and hanging to the back. The bustle consisted of two long strips of cloth with feathers sewn onto it. When he danced, the bustle resembled the tail feathers of a bird. The tail feathers of the "píško," the night hawk, in flight, dark and light feathers trailing behind the powerful bird, that is what my father looked like. He carried in his right hand a small rattle. When he danced his movements resembled that of a bird, quick and sure. His strong legs thrust forward, low to the ground, anchoring his lanky frame. He moved deliberately.

In those days, no one did anything alone, everything was done communally, as a family. In my family, we were all dancers, my mother included. In my extended family, my aunts and uncles were dancers as well. We participated in many dances, and became performers for the public in places where there were many wašícu. I did not always dance, but I traveled with them, as they performed here and there. My father took my mother and me.

In various places they sent for them. "Škál ománi," we say, "Playing they traveled." Regardless of bad weather and extreme cold, they would gather their things and go to camp wherever they were summoned. I was the only girl in the family, so I traveled with my father and mother. They never left me behind but kept me with them.

There were many of us. We all toured together. I had two uncles and they brought their wives with them. My uncles came with us, my father's brother, Sįté, or Tail, and my father's half-brother, whose name was Hupú Chąsákala, or Swallow. My father's half-brother was close to my father, and he traveled with us. "Thí wichó," meaning "his whole family," including their children, came with us.

My uncle Sįté, or Tail, brought his sons with him. His sons were drummers and singers. They came with us and performed, too. They were good singers. In his later life, Sįté's son, my cousin Jackson Tail, performed as a singer in the movie *A Man Called Horse*. He was the Indian man who sat in the corner and sang. He toured with us when we were both younger, and my father, Thatháka Nážį, and his father, Sįté, performed for others.

The men in the family stayed and performed together. We women did the same. The dancing that my father and the other men did, they did in a unified and straightforward manner. It was all done to honor all of the people, not just one dancer or one person. They did not compete. They did what the people had always done, "wachípi," they danced.

In the old ways, the people did not compete in dancing contests. There were no such things. "Tohą́ niyákhe, wachí kį lé oyáte Lakhóta tháwapi cha awą́glakapi," since the beginning of time, these dances belonged to the Lakota people. It was up to them to oversee or look after them, and men like my father and his brothers did. In everything they did, "ehą́k'ehą wó'echų," they honored the old ways.

Thatháka Nážį was a Pheží Mignáka Wachi, or Grass Dancer. My father danced this special dance in the center, for all the people to see, "Ikpázo," we say, "He showed himself," and the people saw him. That was the way he danced. He felt obligated to do it right.

When I was a child, my father was "ithą́cha," he was the "one in charge," when he traveled with his troupe. We went to many places in Nebraska, and to Wyoming, where we danced at the Cheyenne Frontier Days. In Cheyenne, my father and other men rode horses in the events "Lakhól iglúza," while they were dressed in traditional clothes.

He was summoned to Farwell in central Nebraska and he took his dance troupe. We traveled there with his brother, Sité, and half-brother, Swallow. My father took men and women dancers. I was among the children they took with them to dance. My hair was long and I dressed in the "Lakhól," the traditional way. We stayed there four days and performed.

We toured through other towns in Nebraska, including Martin, Broken Bow, and Scottsbluff. One day we were dancing in Martin, my father, mother, and I, when we were asked to go to Broken Bow, where we stayed for a week. They treated us well there. They fed us daily and paid us.

In Scottsbluff, Nebraska, there is a large bluff near where they held the dances. There were many dances there. I danced, too, during our tour. I danced with the young girls they brought with them. I never danced at home when we were on the reservation. At home, I was a spectator but never a dancer.

My mother and the other women dressed "Lakhól chuwígnaka," in traditional dresses, when they danced. These "chuwígnaka," these dresses, were some-times beaded or were called "wamáka chuwígnaka," meaning "animal skin dress." "Upíhaska úpi," they wore other long dresses. The women wore these and danced. In the center they danced. They did not move around like the men, "Owážigžila nážipi," they stood in one spot and they danced. "Oká'owiň," in a circle, they danced. "Ipsíl wachípi," in a jumping manner, they danced. "Yuphíya," in a good manner, they moved.

The men did move when they danced. In the center, "chokáta," they danced for all to see. "Iglúhomnimni," turning this way and that, the men danced. If you look out on the prairie, early in the morning, you will see birds of many kinds. The loudest of these, early in the morning, is the meadowlark, the "thašíyagnupa" as we know it. The most interesting is the prairie grouse, the "šiyó" as we call it. Sometimes, you might even see the rhythmic movement

168

of the "wąblígleška," the spotted eagle, as it circles the sky. In our dances, it is the gracefulness of these birds, whether it was the odd head movements of the prairie grouse or the gracefulness of the hawk or eagle, that the men imitated, for it was said, long ago when the world was first created, that we were made relatives to the birds.

The women did not go running among the men when they danced. "Iglú'oniha," they were expected to conduct themselves in a respectful manner. They stood in one spot and faced the men as they danced. They danced in the same way to all the different songs. They had no special dances like the men. They danced to the Omáha lowápi when they sang the Omaha songs, the honoring songs, or whatever the men danced to, but always in the same way, firmly rooted and proud.

In a respectful manner we all conducted ourselves. "Tuwéni hél mníšica yatkį na chokáta šką waníce," that is, it was unheard of to have someone drink "mníšica," meaning "bad water," our word for alcohol, and perform in the circle, in the center. Who we were, our honor, depended on how we conducted ourselves individually and collectively. A person's behavior in the center, for all to see, reflected on all of us. He would not be acting on his own, but would be representing all of us.

We young girls sat and watched the dancing. We were spectators. We didn't leave the older women for fear of being accused of flirting or other improper behavior. I was self-conscious even then, I did not want to do anything to offend anyone, so I sat and watched the dancing with my mother or grandmother Turtle Lung Woman.

As I grew older, I listened carefully to the words to the songs they were singing. "Wąchíyąka wachį na, ecíyatąhą wa'ú," "I wanted to see you, so on your side I come." A young man might sing this to a young woman as he danced. It was the way things were then, nothing was overt, or aggressive, even in the way the people sang to one another, especially in the way they showed themselves in these dances. In time I understood that even when we were not encouraged to be overt, in their songs to us, the young men flirted with us, and we danced to their songs.

In those days, no matter what they did, the people were careful. It was a way of life to be cautious. They looked after everything that belonged to them. They cared about things that were theirs. These dances and songs were a part of who they were. "Yuhá škátapišni," they did not take these things lightly. They did not play with them carelessly, as children might do. They did not want to lose them through their dishonor.

Song of the Strong-Heart Society

Kholá	Friend
tuwá	whoever
naphé cįhą́	flees
óphaktešni ye	shall not
	participate

21

My Father's Dreadful Dream

When I was five years old, "atéwaye kį hé wíȟable wą theȟíka yuhá," my father, Thatȟáka Nážį, had a dreadful dream. The word "theȟíka," meaning "difficult," was something that only the strong can bear. My father was a solid man, but the dream he had filled him with dread, and for a long time he tried to deny that he had the dream.

"Atéwaye kį hé wíȟable wą yuhá na, wakįyą iwíchahable cha," my father had a dream about Wakįyą, the sacred thunder being. The name Wakįyą means "wakȟą," or "sacred," and "kiyą," "a being that flies."

Wakįyą is a being without form, only those who dream of it can see it. They say it lives at the edge of the world, to the west. It resembles a bird with wide wings, large talons, and a sharp beak. It is a headless creature with an eye that angrily pierces through the clouds. Its glance is lightning; its call is thunder. Indeed its voice is the sound of the drum, a pleasing sound to all spirits.

Wakįyą has a double nature, like all living things, and is capable of destroying as well as nourishing life and making things grow. It brings rain, but just as quickly, without warning, it can bring hail. The sound of hail is like the rattle that the medicine men use to ward off the evil spirits. The drum and rattle, Wakįyą's sounds, are used in any ceremony, one to entice the spirits and the other to ward off the malevolent ones.

It is said that to dream of Wakįyą is to experience terror. Once you dream of him they say your fear turns you foolish. You become "heyókha" and live as a fool. The way my father, Thatȟáka Nážį, began to feel dread when the clouds began to gather for a storm. A feeling he could not control. "Wakįyą o'úkiya chạ," so that when Wakįyą came, Thatȟáka Nážį sometimes fell into a panic.

When the thunder being came, when he arrived, or even when he was in the vicinity, Thatȟáka Nážį appeared visibly shaken and distressed in an unexplainable way. "Iyótiyekiye," he tried to endure, but suffered anyway. "Eš tȟa'įšniya í, tuktógnašna iyá," he would vanish; he would flee. Where he went I did not know. "Tha'įšniya," without a trace he would disappear.

"Ho hé tóna khiglí eyá kú khe," several times while he was riding home in his wagon, a storm would blow in from the northwest. He could see it coming cross the wide-open prairie. We traveled by wagon back then, "ųkúpi echúȟa," while we were traveling the storm would come upon us and my father would go into a panic and flee.

I don't know if my father was seeking a "ȟatéša," a cedar tree, when he ran away. For it was said that Wakįya's power did not work on a cedar tree; one who sought refuge under a cedar tree would not be harmed by Wakįya. For this reason, when a person wanted Wakįya's help, he would take dry fronds from the cedar tree and burn it. Wakįya loved the smell of the smoke from the cedar tree, it was said. Indeed it is a pleasing smell.

This happened several times. When we rode somewhere in our wagon and I noticed a storm coming, my father began to worry. He worried when even a small cloud appeared in the sky, for it was said that Wakįya used the clouds as robes to hide himself; concealed this way he traveled quickly. "Wakįya aglí na maȟpíya wą cík'ala wąyáke kheš," it didn't matter, when they came, even a small cloud would cover Wakįya and transport him anywhere.

When a "maȟpíya," meaning "cloud," even the shadow of one, appeared in the sky, "Héchiya hothú kį cha naȟ'ú khe," Thatȟáka Nážį said, "Wakįya made terrible noises inside of it." He heard it distinctly coming from the cloud. The size of the cloud or the intensity of the storm did not matter. "Ho chána šna, héchiyatą wakȟá lená heyápi chą," he said he heard sacred voices speak in a language foreign to him. He thought he could understand what they were saying, certainly, what they seemed to be implying, but he was too afraid.

"Hothú chą naȟ'ú khe," the sacred voices cried out in anger. He heard it.

"Hothú," as a buffalo bellows, the thunder being called out. Thatháka Nážį heard, but in the beginning he ignored what they said. He chose not to listen. He acted as if the voices were calling for someone else.

He denied what it would mean for him, should he choose to hear what they were saying. He did not believe it was meant for him to hear and obey. "Okáȟniǧešni," he did not want to comprehend it. For this, he suffered for a long time.

"Ho cháṇa šna," so it came to pass, "héchiyaṭa wakhá kį lé hiyúyapi háṭa," when the thunder being sent forth one of his own, he punished Thatháka Nážį. When it came down from the sky, the sacred being, a bolt of lightning sought out Thatháka Nážį. When it found him, "kat'ápi," it struck him and knocked him unconscious.

"Théhąhą gliȟpá," when it struck, Thatháka Nážį was thrown far, for quite a distance. My father fell from the wagon. "Kaktókhiya," way over there. Once, it came while we were riding in our wagon, it struck him and threw him to the ground. He lay there senseless. It happened many times.

"Hąkéya ektáni maké," I did not want to see it, after a while. I became afraid and when they traveled by wagon I stayed at home. "Ináwaye kį kichí la," so he and my mother would travel alone. I was too afraid. I did not understand what it meant. Sometimes my oldest brother, Zįtkála Ská, would travel with him to try to help him.

I remember one of the times this happened. "Áta istó hená áta mark yápi," when he came home, my father's arms appeared as if the sacred beings had painted him in a mysterious way. You could see how they marked him. "Eš héchel ú," still my father endured, all the while denying the dream and refusing to do as it dictated.

"Na héchel ų na," he lived this way. "Waná líla théhą kakíže," for a long time he suffered. "Eyá líla wókiyakapi," the elders tried to talk to him about what this meant. My grandmother Turtle Lung Woman and others tried to tell him. They tried to speak to him many times about his suffering, but he would not listen. It wasn't that he was skeptical about the things they told him, it was that he chose not to comprehend what it meant. His fear was too overwhelming. The way it was said: To dream of Wakíyą was to know terror. My father knew.

"Wóchekiye khó hél áya na," Turtle Lung Woman even took him to ceremonies where they prayed for him. "Hél áya na eš," his relatives brought him to ceremonies, still he would not heed their words or do as he was instructed. "Echú chíšni," he did not want to do what they told him to do. He dreaded the thought of doing as the sacred beings instructed.

"Waná líla echá kakíže," thus Thatháka Ná̇žį suffered for a long time. "Kakíže," he endured great hardship. "Tóna khiglé Wakíyą aglí na okísota chą́na šna," many times the thunder being came and when it emptied itself, it dissipated. As young as I was I knew my father had suffered through another storm.

The times we came home in our wagon when the sacred beings came, and how they threw him down, off of the wagon, as if he were an insignificant thing. "Khúta yuȟpápi, hená khúta yuȟpápi khe," a man like my father was thrown from the wagon, a good distance, like an ant blown off of a blade of grass by a strong wind.

It was not only Thatháka Ná̇žį who suffered. The rest of us could only watch helplessly as he wrestled with what the thunder beings were asking him to do. We knew his suffering came from his own denial. When he chose not to listen, "khúta kaktókhi kaȟ'ól iyápi khe," they threw him down, way over there, like an insect in the wind. It was that way for a long time. "Eyá héchekceca," that's how it went until finally my father listened to the old people and the medicine men. They told him to do the Chéȟ'ohomni Wachí, the Circle the Kettle Dance. It was what Thatháka Ná̇žį needed to do to appease Wakíyą.

Friend

Kholá	Friend
wąmáyąka yo	behold
wakhą́	sacred
makáǧa pelo	I have been made
kholá	friend
wąmáyąka yo	behold
wakhą́yą	sacred
makáǧa pelo	I have been made
maȟpíya	at the gathering of the clouds
oglínažįta	before a thunderstorm

22

Kettle Dance

Thatháka Nážį, my father, was told that Wakíyą would leave him alone if he sacrificed a "šúkala," a young dog, less than ten weeks old. A šúkala is a "wahóši," or "messenger," and exits the world through the west to tell Wakíyą that Thatháka Nážį has had a dream and grows sick from it. It was said that Wakíyą is the patron of increase, nourishment, and growth and will hear the šúkala and help Thatháka Nážį get well again.

The old ones like Turtle Lung Woman were alive when Thatháka Nážį had his dream, and they made a ceremony for him. A "wakhá wicháša," a holy man, told him to sacrifice the šúkala. "Echél yaníkte, khe," he told him, "If you do this, you will be healed." He did as he was told, but he still suffered.

He went to the wakhá wicháša again, who told him he had to do the Chéłi'ohomni Wachí, the Circle the Kettle Dance. "Tóškhe echúkte kį, okíyakapi," he told him what to do. The grave event that was to occur made everyone apprehensive. The solemn way in which my father sought to procure his own healing was indeed sad. My father wanted healing, to be free of his suffering. We all wanted it for him. I was very young and did not fully understand it. My mother, Turtle Lung Woman, and all of our relatives did. They cried, wailing and lamenting on the day my father was to perform the ceremony.

On a given day, in the spring of the following year after his dreadful dream, my father made known his intention to fulfill his obligation. On that day, before the ceremony began, "wasú kic'ú na," he undressed and stood ready. When they began to sing, he danced. He approached in this manner, dancing in a mysterious way. He danced toward a "chéǧa," or "kettle," that stood in the center. He danced around it. As he did this, he went among the people, deliberately approaching some. It was said that those he approached had dreams of the Heyókha and became ill from it. Those men sat in the ceremony and he approached them individually. When he did, each one became visibly anxious, "naphápi," they fled.

He danced along the edge of the circle where the people sat on the ground, visually inspecting those present. He approached each Heyókha dreamer, and when the dreamer fled, he moved on. When he saw all those present, he stood apart in the center and began dancing toward the chéǧa.

Although I was a small child, I sensed the sadness around me. I heard wailing and felt it deep inside. All the while, my father danced around the kettle. He danced around it, circling it, the way one circles an enemy. While he danced, he danced this way and that. In a mysterious way, "glakíkiya wachí," the way only a Heyókha dreamer dances.

While he moved this way, he reached into the boiling liquid in the kettle and pulled out the head of the four-legged, the šúkala. He took it out and held it for all to see. Meanwhile, four men we call Tokhála, meaning "foxes," sat in the center near the kettle. They held their hands like pistols, the way a young boy does, they feigned shooting him, as he danced by, turning himself this way and that in a mysterious way. When he passed them, they bent low, took aim, and shot him. In the old days they say Wakíya's weapons were the spear and war club. The Tokhála, imitating Wakíya, used pistols, the new weapon, to feign killing him. Ignoring them, my father danced closer and closer to the people sitting in the circle.

They said the Tokhála, the four men, were selected to ladle out the soup in the kettle. When my father reached in and took out the "phá," the head of the "hutópa," he ran along the circle where the people sat. He took a small piece of the sacred meat and gave it to those who were ill. They ate it to be well, the way he was doing this to be healed. He went throughout the circle and came around with the phá, and when he completed the circle, he returned to the kettle and prayed.

A song that is sung when this is done goes like this: "Kholá, wamáyaka yo, wakhą makáǧa pelo." It is a song for all those present: "Friends, behold, sacred I have been made." It was so, for the people said that those who dreamed of Wakį́yą would know great honor.

It healed him. He did one thing, from that time forward, when a thunderstorm approached. "Wakį́yą ukíye," we say, when the sacred beings were on their way. When they approached, someone would ask my father, "Tókhakta he?" They wanted to know if the storm would be a bad one. He would answer, "It comes, but do not fear. Prepare for it. It might rain on us, but it goes elsewhere."

Thathą́ka Ną́žį knew the power of Wakį́yą and respected it. He burned the dry fronds from the cedar tree to gain his favor. He kept the dry cedar nearby, and when a thunderstorm approached he lit a match and threw it into a tin bowl containing the dry fronds. The match lit the dry cedar, and after a minute or so, he would blow out the flame and watch the cedar smolder. The smell of the smoke clears the tension in the air before the storm. It calmed Thathą́ka Ną́žį.

When he did this, he released the spirit of the cedar tree, the favorite "chą́," the favorite tree, of Wakį́yą. In his mind Thathą́ka Ną́žį sought refuge in the smoke of the cedar. His spirit and that of the tree joined together when he breathed in the smoke of the chą́, they joined together to please Wakį́yą.

He would say about the impending storm, "It is nothing to create hardship for anyone, nothing to make anyone sad," perhaps the way he grew sad when he was ill. In the time before he was healed, he heard them speaking inside the clouds and grew fearful. After his healing, he did not consider himself sacred, or special, but he knew the sacred language they spoke when a thunderstorm approached, and he was no longer afraid. He saw Wakį́yą as benign; a spirit that governed "maȟpíya," the clouds, and "maǧážu," the rain, no longer malevolent.

I saw many Chéȟ'ohomni Wachí, or Circle the Kettle Dances, as I grew older. Just as they say Wakį́yą is many in one, there are many dreamers, both men and women, who experienced different aspects of the same dreadful dream. In these dreams they say they see the colors black, red, or blue but the symbolic color of Wakíya is the color yellow. These colors represent Wakíya in his many forms, thus ceremonies and dreams of Wakíya take many forms.

The old women were the saddest at these events. "Wakícilowapi," they wailed, and did the tremolo. They cherished these ceremonies and showed great respect. In one ceremony I saw them bring an old man into the center. The Tokhála danced and "thaló wąží kazépi hąta," using sharp sticks they stabbed pieces of the sacred meat and approached the old man. He defended himself. He held his hand like a gun and shot at them. But the Tokhála "í ogná khíyapi," they put the sacred meat from the "hutópa" into his mouth. "Hená wóyu'oniha tháka hécha," what they did was a great honor.

It was the way things were done. When the people danced, they began with one of these events. They said it was against the law to do them, but we found a way to keep them hidden, embedded in our social dances, we kept them alive.

PART 3

Death

Song of the Dead Chiefs

Kholá
táku yakhá pelo
itháchą kį
henápila yelo
miyéka kheš echų́ uwáthahe
we

Friend
what you are saying is true
the chiefs
are gone
so
I myself will
try

23

Rations

I remember in the 1930s, at every new moon, the government gave us rations that were surplus government food. It was after the treaties were made between our people and the government that issues of food, clothing, blankets, and other things, like farm implements and seeds, were given to us in return for land we relinquished to the federal government.

In earlier years the government wanted us to "wóžu," to sow or grow seeds, and they gave us seeds and farm implements as well. In those days it was common to see farm implements rusting in the hot sun. They were left where they were put when the government issued them to us. The land they put us on was not good farm land. We knew, although we were naturally not farmers, because we saw good farm land along the Platte River where we went to work in the fields. There we saw all the grasses the wašícu grew. There the land is rich, and irrigation is used to grow the seeds and grasses they brought into our country. On the reservation we lived on dry land where water is scarce but where the buffalo grass stands tall. In the old days, that was all we wanted to keep the buffalo alive. That was all we wanted to get everything we needed to live.

The government brought many things to the reservation to make sure we could live on what they gave us. They built houses and buildings to store all the things they thought we needed. They brought sacks of flour, sugar, beans, and other things. They stored these in buildings. They built corrals for the cattle they brought to give us fresh meat. They tried to give us pork, but we thought it smelled bad. We didn't have a name for many of the things they brought to us. They hired men and their families to come and issue these things to us. Sometimes I wondered if it would have been easier to bring the buffalo back.

In the early years they issued us clothing because we could no longer hunt and use the hides to make our own. In Lakota, "há" means "animal skins," and it also means "clothes." "Íše há kpamní škhe, eháni blanket na'iš wawášteše wicháḱ'up séce," that is, "há," or "clothing" was distributed as well as useful items like blankets. Women were given "dress goods," or bolts of new material to make their own clothing. Sometimes men were given wool suits and hats, coats, and flannel shirts.

While I was growing up I saw them give out food like they do now. I remember around the year 1933 when it was ration day. How everyone came on horses and wagons hitched to horses. They came to take what was being given that day. They brought "wóžuhala," small sacks, that they sewed as containers for carrying home their rations.

"Wótapi echíyata iš," as far as food goes, "wí iyóhila," every new moon, or month, the government gave us flour, coffee, sugar, bacon, and "eyá táku iyúha," whatever else they thought we needed. The coffee came as green coffee beans, and everyone knew how to roast them for their own use. The women all had their own grinders that they turned by hand. They roasted and ground their own coffee. "Wakhályapi" we called it, "heated it is." It is a drink that everyone liked, except me. I never liked it and I never drank it unless I was a guest somewhere and it was offered to me. I didn't refuse it. In our culture, it is considered bad etiquette to refuse food that is given to you.

"Wóžuhala gluhá ye," they say, "Bring your containers." So it was, "watóhal šna," at a certain time each month, we would go to where the "thí ská," a white wooden frame house, stood. It was called "old boss farmer's house," and each "okášpe," or "district," had one. The boss farmer was the district farmer who lived in the white house. The boss farmer's house was the issue station for the government. The boss farmer supervised how the rations were issued in our "okášpe." It was a house that stands north of the trading post.

There they would ration out the food and coffee. "Áta šna yulóchį šna nážįpi," there the people stood in long lines, one behind the other, waiting for their rations. The men in cowboy hats and the women with blankets or shawls wrapped around them. The women still carried their small children the old way, upright in a modified cradle board, carried on the back. The woman carrying her child this way would drape her blanket over the child, covering them both. They looked odd, one body, one blanket, and two heads, a mother and child, both facing forward in the line. Sometimes, the women draped the blanket over their heads. They stood close together in those long lines. It was a time to see everyone and to visit and to catch up on news.

I must have been very young. I saw it. I did not think much about it. "Henáš táku ecámišni," I did not think it was important. Mom-mah, my mother, was an able-bodied woman and she concerned herself with those things. Then, I was a child, I didn't think about what it meant. I went with them and waited in those lines each month.

Now they are all gone, my grandmother, mother, and father, those who stood in those lines with me. "Wahéchetuya kį él úpišni," those from that generation are no longer with us. That "thí ská," the old white house, old boss farmer's house, still stands where I can see it near the Porcupine store. When I look that way, sometimes I feel as I did when I was a child and I stood in those long lines with the men, women, and children. All of us standing or riding on wagons pulled by horses, looking expectantly toward the boss farmer's house. All of us waiting with our "wóžuhala," the containers to carry our rations home.

May This Be the Day

Ạpétu mitháwa k'ụ	May this be
létu	the day
nụwé	I consider mine
wazíyata	from the north
thaté uyé cị	the wind is blowing
ạpétu mitháwa k'ụ	may this be
létu	the day
nụwé	I consider mine

24

"Tąyą́ Wąbláke," Clear Eyes

I had five brothers, and my oldest brother was Zįtkála Ská, White Bird. He would sometimes help Turtle Lung Woman and Kaká Bear Goes in the Wood, when he was alive. He had a Model T Ford, so he would take them wherever they wanted to go. "Wicháyuha," he took care of them. They sat in the back seat of his Model T. Ųcí Turtle Lung Woman wrapped herself in her best blanket for the occasion. Kaká wore his best white shirt buttoned to the chin. He wore suit pants held up neatly with suspenders. They both wore their best moccasins.

My oldest brother, Zįtkála Ská, was born in 1904, and he was in his late twenties when they were alive. His oldest son was close to me in age, he was five years my junior, and he became like a younger brother to me. It was this son that was given one of the last opportunities to "count coup." He did so when a Khąǧí wicháša came to visit our reservation. This man was seated in the center of the old dance hall, and Zįtkála Ská's oldest son was given a coup stick and he touched the Khąǧí wicháša with it. The year was 1935. The older men and women like Turtle Lung Woman remembered how it was with the Khąǧí wicháša.

I spent more time with Turtle Lung Woman after Kaká died in 1930. "Mišnála wįmáyą," I was the only girl in my family. So, "Ųcí kį hé ówakiye," Turtle Lung Woman, my grandmother, and I were inseparable. I followed close behind her. It was the way it was supposed to be between grandmothers and granddaughters, but I was the only granddaughter. "Kichí o'úye," we were companions. "Iyúškįyą kichí wa'ú," we were content that way.

"Tąyą́ wąbláke," I saw her with clear eyes. "Kichíšna makį́ na wéchasto," I sat with her and combed her hair. When I sat with her she spoke to me. "Eháni wóglake." "Eháni," we say, when we speak of a time before now. "Wóglake," or "oyáka," indicating how one tells a story to another. She told me stories.

"Iyúškiya kichí wa'ú," we were happy together. It was not only granddaughters like me who enjoyed special relationships with their grandmothers. In our "ohúkaka," or old stories, there are many stories about grandmothers who helped their grandchildren through magical powers that the "ká," or "old people," are sometimes thought to have.

In one story, Phiyá, a young boy, lived with his grandmother. The word "phiyá" means "to make new." When "phiyá" is used, as in the word "waphíya," it refers to a healer. Phiyá in the "ohúkaka," the story, was born poor like Crazy Horse. Phiyá did not have parents, only his grandmother. As a young boy, Phiyá and his grandmother were driven from the main camp because they were filthy. They were poor and unclean. As he grew, Phiyá asked his grandmother to help him.

His grandmother indeed had supernatural powers that she used to help him when he fell in love with a beautiful girl. The girl's wealthy family did not want her to marry a poor man. A poor dirty man like Phiyá. The grandmother interceded with supernatural powers and the girl agreed to marry him.

In one story Phiyá's grandmother taught him how to talk to birds and animals. He spoke to Kheglézela, Šugmánitu, and Thašíyagnupa, Turtle, Wolf, and Meadowlark, asking them to help him when Thatháka Gnaškíya, or Crazy Buffalo, a mythical beast in our old stories, took Phiyá's wife as a captive. In the story, Phiyá's grandmother asked the turtle, wolf, and meadowlark to help her grandson. She told the turtle that she would give him a thick shell to protect himself if he helped her grandson locate "mní," water. She promised the wolf she would give him thick hair to keep himself warm from the cold winds of Wazíya, the northern spirit, if he imparted his cunning ways to her grandson. She told the meadowlark that she would give him a beautiful voice if he helped her grandson to hide without cover, the way a meadowlark can hide on the prairie. In the story, the turtle, wolf, and meadowlark help Phiyá rescue his wife. They earn the gifts Phiyá promised them.

In these stories, Phiyá's grandmother taught him many things. He became a "waphíye," a healer, in a mysterious way. She told him to come to her if he was ever in trouble and that she would always help him. So it was with Turtle Lung Woman. I was her only granddaughter, like Phiyá, I was close to my grandmother and she taught me many things. I did not learn the mysterious things she knew, the waphíye she had. I do not know if she meant to give to me. When I used to sit with her and comb her hair, she trusted me with many things, most of all, she trusted me with her hair. When I finished combing her hair I would take any hair on the comb and carefully roll it, "kagmígma," in a ball and give it back to her. She would take it and dispose of it properly.

One day Turtle Lung Woman became ill. She was eighty-four years old, by then. I was fifteen years old. She lay in her bed, too ill to move. I remember how she spoke to me, to my mother and father. She instructed us, as she had always done.

She lay there in her blankets, covered to the chin, and she said a medicine man told her that she would see the early spring. Indeed, it was the month we call Phežíša Wí, The Moon When the Red Grass Appears, that she became ill.

In her bed, "wóglag ȟpáya," she spoke as she lay there. She told us to welcome anyone who came to see her. She said to offer coffee or tea to anyone who came, she said, "eyá tuwá thimá hiyú ȟą́ta," meaning "anyone who came into her home." She said to welcome them. The words she used were very specific, as if she had thought a long time about them, perhaps as she lay there.

"Thimá" is a word she used the old way, perhaps the way it was used in that time when she lived in a tipi and made moccasins in the moonlight because Ité Siyákhiya was going to war against the Khaǧí wicháša. "Thimá hiyú we," she would say, "Come into my house." "Thí," meaning her "dwelling," the buffalo hide tipi she called hers in that time when she and the others "wichákicilowąpi," wailed and sang for those who went to war against the Khąǧí wicháša.

The way she said "thimá" felt ancient. "Thí," meaning "my structure," and "ma," meaning "my own" or "belonging to me." It is a word used to mean "my" or "mine." "Thimá," meaning to come inside, through the small opening at the entrance of the tipi. When you enter, you are enclosed, encapsulated by this dwelling I call "mine," or belonging to me. When you enter my home, we are intimately close and connected in my dwelling. This circular dwelling I call mine. It was both an invitation and a statement. Her words always reflected who she was.

At the time we did not know why she expected to see many visitors. She knew they would come when she died. When she finally passed from this world to the spirit world, they came. She died in the early spring of 1935. It was the fifth day of April when she died. She was conscious and aware as she lay in her death bed. "Wachį́ksapa," we say, "with full presence of mind."

When she died she was buried near Kaká Bear Goes in the Wood. They are both buried at St. Julia's Episcopal Church. They lay facing the east, "wíhinapha étkiya," in the direction where the sun rises. Kaká's gravestone is prominent on the hillside. He earned it as a scout for the army, it signifies who he is. Turtle Lung Woman has no monument, only the earth that was as it had been before she was buried there, remaining seemingly untouched. There is nothing to mark where she is buried.

I stayed close to my mother after Turtle Lung Woman died. "Héhą wąbláke," I saw Turtle Lung Woman then. I can still see her now. "Wóglake kį óta weksúye," many of the things she said, I remember. "Ehą́ni wóglake, ehą́ni, kákhiya héktakiya wichó'ų kį hé chékiya wóglake," she spoke of a time before now, way back, when the people lived a certain way.

When she died, her "wóphiye," her medicine bag, was not placed in the "wicháȟapi ognáke," meaning "the chest in which men or women are buried," the

196

coffin she was put into. "Théha paháta, tuktél égnakapi. Naku yuhá ḣpáyapišni. Naku tókhiyab wakátuya glo'íyab škhe hená," her medicine bag and all the sacred things she had were taken far into the hills, as far back as one could go, and they were left there, out in the open. It was said that her spirit came for them before it made its journey home.

Song of Pretended Search

Ecá	I wonder
tukté	where
thípi so	they live

25

"Ąpétu kį hél," On a Given Day, I Became a Woman

One day, I was getting ready for school. I was in sixth grade at the "day school." We called it the day school because it was different from the boarding school where other children were sent. My family kept me home, and I attended the day school.

There were no school buses, and old man Pumpkin Seed used to pick me up in his horse and wagon. He would pull up to the wagon road leading to our house, and I would climb into the back of the old buckboard with his daughters. His daughters went to the same school, and he would give us girls a ride to school. Sometimes the boys would try to hitch a ride on his wagon, and he would use his long horse whip to scare them off. I don't know why but old man Pumpkin Seed disliked the boys and made it known to everyone that he would only give certain girls a ride in his wagon. I was lucky to be one of those girls.

That day, before I left for school, I decided to use the outhouse. While I was there, I noticed that I was bleeding from a place I didn't expect. "Ináwaye kį wakípą na wachéye," I shouted for my mother and began to cry. My mother came and tried to assure me that it was not unnatural that this should occur.

I thought there was something wrong with me. I was the only girl in my family, I did not have any sisters or older women to tell me about these things. My mother didn't tell me. Turtle Lung Woman did not concern herself with these things, and I didn't know what it meant. I thought I was dying. "Hiyá," "No," my mother said. "Hé wįníyą cha waná héchetu we," "You are a woman, thus it is so," she said. She assured me that there was nothing wrong with me.

"Wíyą iyóhila héchų kšto," she said, "All women go through the same thing."

"Tasé lé táku wąží šícašni," she said emphatically, "It is not a terrible thing that is happening to you. It is just the way it is."

She then told me to sit still while she and my oldest brother Zįtkála Ská's wife, Jessie, made preparations for me to show me what I had to do. "Táku mniȟúha yuhá hiyú na, ecékchel micáǧab," they brought me some cloths to make the things I was to wear. They took me inside to a room where I sat alone thinking about what was happening to me. I did not go to school that day, nor did I go to school for the next four days while I was this way. On the first day, I stayed home and waited for my parents who had gone somewhere. It seemed like I sat there for a long time. Finally they came home.

My mother and father brought home an older woman. A woman like Turtle Lung Woman who was past menopause and able to help in these matters. It was the way my parents thought it should be, that she explain certain things to me. Her last name was Scout. She was Louis Scout's mother. She had a dream and practiced the ways of a medicine woman.

In a quiet way, Winúȟcala, Old Woman, Scout spoke to me. She told me all the things my mother thought I should know. She explained the significance of what was happening to me. She then did for me as my parents instructed her to, an Išnáthi Awíchalową, a ceremony for women who must live alone for a while. "Išnáthi," meaning "she lives alone," and "awíchalową," meaning "they sing for her." The ceremony itself is an old one. It was the way all of these mysteries were explained, the way a young girl became a woman.

In this ceremony, the first thing Old Woman Scout did was to take some dry sage, which she carefully rolled into small bundles that burned easily. "Pheží ȟóta ų eyá azílmaye na," she took the "gray grass," the sage, burned it, and put the fire out, letting it smolder in a small tin pan. She walked around me, moving the tin pan up and down so that the smoke from the sage covered every part of me. She prayed as she purified me this way. It was said that Thaté, Wind, lives in the spirit of the sage. Its scent is strong like the wind on the prairie, the evil spirits flee from it.

My father kept an "iníthi," a purification lodge, nearby. What the wašícu or white people call a "sweat lodge." This is a misnomer since the ceremony does not focus on "themní," or "sweat," but on the word "ní," meaning "spirit." The iníthi is a place where a Lakota goes to make his or her "ní," or "spirit," strong. The word "iní-thi" is a two-part word, so "iní" refers to this ritual of purifying the body and making the spirit strong. The other part, "thí," refers to the structure or place where this is done.

The ritual of purifying the spirit is called an Iníkağe, a Purification Ceremony performed in the iníthi. It is our oldest and most sacred ceremony. It is done before anything out of the ordinary is done by anyone.

My father's purification lodge was a small circular structure, built close to the ground. It stood approximately four feet high. It was made with young branches from a willow tree. About sixteen of these were placed in the ground in a circle measuring about six feet for a small lodge and even bigger for a larger one. These branches are bent to form a circle and are tied in the center. Over this are placed blankets, and in the old days, buffalo robes, to form a circular hut.

A hole is dug in the middle of the structure to put rocks that are heated in a fire. The hole measures about two feet wide and two feet deep. The bottom of the hole is lined with hot rocks for the ceremony. The rocks are heated in a fire outside. A fire tender, usually a man, takes care of it for the people in the purification lodge. He builds it several hours before the ceremony begins. When the ceremony starts he brings in the hot stones, the number depending on how many the medicine man or woman conducting the ceremony needs. He brings them in through an opening on the east side of the lodge where the entrance is.

We prepared ourselves to enter the iníthi, just the older woman and I. We women did not participate with the men, our modesty prevented us from entering the same iníthi as the men. It was said in the old days the men were afraid of us during this time when we had our menses because they felt we had power over them.

We women held our own ceremony, which is in all respects the same as the men. We hold our own because, as in all things, we Lakota women were separate in the way we conducted ourselves and our lives. We women even had our own language to express the things that were important to us. The men also had their own languages, an ordinary one and a sacred one.

The men feared us during this time in our lives when we had our menses. They felt that we released a "thú," a power, that was stronger than theirs. We were able to impart this "thú" and negate theirs, and they were afraid of being affected in any way. It was not that we were "impure" during this time, it was that we were mysterious in an unexplainable way, and it was thought that we were able to influence the men in a way they feared.

So, Old Woman Scout and I entered my father's iníthi, just the two of us. She wore a thin cotton dress and wrapped a thin blanket around herself. I wore the same with a blanket wrapped around. Initially, she entered alone, taking her "chanúpa wakhá," her sacred pipe, with her. She took it and prayed with it, purifying the iníthi with sweet grass, which is a smell the spirits love. She used sage after the sweet grass, to make sure only the good spirits entered the iníthi.

She brought out the pipe she used and placed it upon a mound outside. This mound we call Ųcí Makhóche, Grandmother Earth. She placed it with the stem of her sacred pipe facing "wiyóhiyapa," toward the east where the sun rises, as the name implies. She brought out the pipe four times during the ceremony. Each time it faced one of the four sacred directions: "wiyóhiyapa," the east; "itókaǧa," the south; "wiyóȟpeyata," the west; and "wazíyata," the north. It is how the ceremony is done.

When she finished her preparations, she took me into the iníthi. We entered together, just the older woman and I. It was like entering a dark cave with the light entering from the east, where the entrance was. She entered first and sat "chatkúta," or "in the place of honor," on the west side, opposite the entrance. The floor of the lodge was lined with "pheží ȟóta," or "gray grass," sage. We sat on this soft blanket of sage with our legs demurely tucked under us, to the right. I sat opposite from her and watched as the man tending the fire began to bring in hot rocks from the fire. He began to fill the hole with the glowing rocks. The dry heat from the rocks warmed my face as I waited patiently.

Old Woman Scout first asked for seven sacred ones from the fire keeper. She wanted four for the four directions, two for the sky and earth, and the seventh one for Tákuškąšką, the Creator, or Šką, as they call Him in the sacred language. She called for a few more stones after the seven, and then the fire keeper, "anáthake" we say, he closed the flaps. The number of rocks brought into the center of the iníthi vary for the men and women. The men took anywhere from seven to twenty-eight, but for us, we took less than that. When the fire keeper closed the entrance to the iníthi, darkness entered and I was apprehensive.

I sat with the blanket wrapped around me, covering myself even in the darkness. Old Woman Scout had a small metal bucket of water with a dipper in it. She took the water in the dipper and sprinkled the stones with the water four times, praying as she did so: To the four sacred directions, to the earth she prays, then to the sky, and to Tákuškąšką. The room filled with steam. She continued to pray. After she prayed and the steam settled upon us both, she took a deep breath and began to sing. Her prayers and songs invoked the spirits, asking them to come to her aid. It was said, long ago, that the evil spirits were afraid when the people sang. In all of our ceremonies, songs are sung before beginning anything important. She paused after singing, in the quiet of the dark lodge, and she spoke to me.

What I remember about my first Iníkağe, or Purification Ceremony, was the intense heat. Inside the iníthi, it was all vapor, like a spirit, I sat in the fog, unable to see. The steam reached into me, deep inside where my most human self lives. "Khowákiphe," I was afraid. In my fear, I felt like a small infant, cradled by the steam. The old woman told me not to be afraid, that at any time she would open the flaps to the iníthi, if I let her know. I was determined not to be afraid, as young as I was, I knew it was not right to fear it.

Initially I was not aware of anyone but myself. After a while, I was less preoccupied with myself and listened intently for Old Woman Scout's voice. Finally, it was coherent. She had been praying, singing, and speaking all along.

I did not hear her voice before, I was listening to all the sounds in the iníthi that made me apprehensive at first. Like the sound the hot stones made when she poured the cold water over them. It was said that the hot stones helped to free the spirit of the water. It becomes vapor in the iníthi that we breathe; it enters us and makes us stronger.

In the iníthi we celebrate the spirit of water. It was said that the spirit of the water is good for the ní of humankind. It is this, the spirit of water as seen in the steam that purifies. It enters the body when one breathes it in during the ceremony. It enters and cleanses the human body. It exits the body when a person wipes away the "themní," the sweat. The themní carries away any or all impurities. It was what a medicine man believed, too, when he treated a sick person. The first thing a medicine man would do to heal the person would be to put him through an Iníkaǧe.

When I released my fear, I heard Old Woman Scout speak. I remember her words. It was her duty, she said, as requested by my parents, to instruct me. "Wįmáyą cha táku tókhel wakínicąkte hená áta ųspémakhiye," she said I was now a woman. She told me she would try to teach me the things I needed to know. She instructed me in practical matters like how I should conduct myself during the time I had the woman's illness.

She told me that for a period of four days I was to conduct myself in a quiet and respectful manner. "Óhą hiyúšni ye," she said in the feminine voice, "Stay away from people." She talked of many things and she told me that from this time forward I must always be mindful of how I conducted myself. "Tákuni apsícešni ye, eyá, chéǧa na'įš tákuni, eh," she said, "Do not walk over anything, especially pots that we cook with or anything else."

She told me I should isolate myself, remaining as still as possible. She told me to keep myself busy with beadwork or sewing, but nothing physically active. She told me that long ago when we lived "wichálakhóta úpi," in the traditional way, women like Turtle Lung Woman would sit and quietly do quillwork, bead-work, or make moccasins, but now things are not the same. In my time, I would be given a sewing kit and "pieces" of material cut for patterns for quilts.

"Wíyąkhošma heháta thiyómata makį na wawákaǧe na'įš táku," she told me, as soon as I noticed that my time had come and my menses began, I should commence with busy work, perfecting my sewing or beading. She said I should find a place away from people and work quietly. "Wahókumakhiye," she taught me these things, she said to learn them well.

She told me that I was to properly dispose of the bundles I used to keep myself clean. She said to keep them away from everyone else. I was the only person who should touch them. She reflected a fear that the people had in the old days when it was said that some old medicine men took the first menstrual flow of a young woman and used it in strange ways, to sometimes make love medicine for a young man so he could coerce a young woman into a relationship.

She said to avoid the company of men, to refrain from walking in front of them or near them. "Wichíthokabkab iyáyešni ye," she said, "Do not parade yourself in front of them." If there were men gathered somewhere in a public place or even in my own household, my own father, brothers, or other male relatives, I must not walk in front of them at this time, as a sign of respect.

The things she said about men, I thought I understood. I had known for a while that I was physically maturing. What she was telling me was for my own protection, I knew. I had to be careful and aware of how I conducted myself in their presence. I was now able to bear children and I must be aware of this great responsibility. She wanted me to learn these things well.

A medicine woman can see into the future, it is said. Old Woman Scout said she saw good things in my future. She told me, "Thokátakiya wichó'icháǧe wąží wašté ánikte." "Thokáta," meaning "in a time yet to come," "wichó'icháǧe," signifying "a generation," "ánikte," meaning "you will take." She said I would take into the future a generation that would do good things for the people.

When we finished the Iníkaǧe, I understood some of the things she told me. She explained them in the old way, in the old language. She gave expression to things I cannot explain, many things I thought I could understand, other things that I could only dream about. She helped me to understand my connection to the cycles of the moon. How the full moon gives power to the sacred. She spoke of things female and filled with mystery. She called the moon Uçí, Grandmother, the way we called the earth Uçí Makhóche, Grandmother Earth.

My own mother spoke to me during this time, I listened and tried to do what I was taught. By and by I finished my first "išnáthi," meaning "alone she lives," signifying this time. I sat alone and when I was done with the four days, "amá'ipi cha," they took me back to the same place to see Old Woman Scout.

She took the "pheží ȟóta," or "gray grass," and heated it, and washed me with it. She patiently wiped me clean with the warm water and sage. Once I was purified, I was able to rejoin my family as before. It was the way I lived from that time forward, practicing the things I was taught in my first Iníkaǧe.

A Buffalo Said to Me

Wahínawaphį kte   I will appear
wąmáyąka yo   behold me
thatháka wą   a buffalo
hemákiya   said to me

26

Buffalo Ceremony

In the 1930s, a round dance hall was built near Porcupine Creek, right below where the water tower is near the school. It was built in an area situated between the bends of the meandering creek. The trees along the creek sheltered it from the strong winds. A natural spring nearby provided drinking water for the people who came to camp there for dances or other events. There were shallow places in the creek where the horses could walk in and drink.

The hall was a round log house built for dances and other social gatherings. It was large and allowed room for a good number of dancers. The base of the house was made of logs, and the roof over it consisted of branches covered with dirt. A large hole was left in the center.

I know other communities had them. We called them "owáchi miméla," round dance halls. It was there in that place near where my aunt Lizzie Little Boy used to live that my mother and father had a ceremony for me. They invited many people who came and camped there in a clearing where the "owáchi miméla" was.

Shortly after I had finished my "išnáthi," or "alone she dwells" ceremony, my mother and father surprised me with an event I had not expected. I returned to school, and my days seemed normal again. Then one day I noticed that my mother and father were making preparations for an event. Pah-pah and Mom-mah were in my father's truck and were preparing to leave.

"Tókhiya láb he? ephé," I asked my mother, "Where are you going?" "Léchiya Tuthill héchi, tha lessee héchi ptégleška wą hiyó'ųyapikte," Mom-mah answered, "We are going to Tuthill to your father's lessee to get a cow he has for us." "Cha, táku tókhaŋųkta he?" I asked, "So what are you going to do?" Mom-mah did not answer.

The next day, "owáchi tȟaní hél," where the old dance hall was, "ahí wichóthi," many people came and camped. They came because my mother and father invited them to a ceremony to be held for me. "Miyé cha Thatȟáka olówapi, hécha ma'úkte škhe," I was to have a Thatȟáka Lowápi Wó'echu, a Buffalo Ceremony. A ceremony for young girls when they reach womanhood.

A long time ago, in a time before now, young women like me had this ceremony to signify that we were from the Pté Oyáte, the Buffalo People. In our stories it was told how we Lakotas first became Pté Oyáte: A young Lakota man brought home a young woman from the west. This dark-haired woman with large nostrils was the first Buffalo Woman. Her union with the young man brought the sacred Buffalo People to us. They came from the west, where they lived under the world, where the sun went to rest. In our stories it was said that, at an earlier time, we also emerged from that place under the world.

The Buffalo People were as relatives to us. They gave themselves to us so that we would always have an abundance of food. Since then, the buffalo is seen as the patron of provision and hospitality, as well as supervisor of ceremonies. It was they who taught us to do the Wiwáyag Wachípi, the Sun Dance. The spirit of the buffalo protected young women, mothers, and children. So it was, my parents wanted a ceremony to ensure my well-being as a chaste young woman.

The cow Pah-pah and Mom-mah brought home was killed. It was to provide fresh meat, the way buffalo meat was used in our old ceremonies and feasts. "Pté kté na áta ok'óke," the cow was butchered and many preparations were made. It was a "wó'echu," a celebration or event marking the significance of what had happened to me, my first menses.

The celebration was held at the old dance hall. It began in the morning and continued into the night with feasting and dancing. "Ináwaye kị wíȟpeya," my mother practiced a certain ritual. "Wíȟpeya," she "gave away" many valuable gifts to the guests. She gave away blankets, shawls, and other valuable things that she had been saving for this occasion. She displayed these things in the center of the circle first, for everyone to see and admire, in the same way a fine feast is set before the people. Then she gave them as gifts to the guests. My mother and father displayed great generosity in the feast and "wíȟpeya." It was the way it had always been done. We Lakotas have always enjoyed honorable acts of generosity and displays of goodwill toward others.

An "éyapaha," or "herald," announced all the things that my mother and father wanted him to. He stood in the center, where all the people gathered could hear him. He made announcements for my parents. The éyapaha, usually a man, summoned special guests, whom my parents identified in advance, to the center. Those guests, summoned by name, entered the circle where I stood in the center with my parents. When the time came each guest approached us, shook our hands individually, my parents and I, and accepted our gift. We gave generously. The more we gave, the more honored I was.

At a special time during the event, my parents asked through the éyapaha, "Tónapi he?" They asked, "How many young women were present who had gone through this ceremony?" My parents wanted to know. If they had been though this ceremony the herald told them to come and join me in the center.

   In the old days a song of pretended search would have been sung for me and the young girls who were to join me. "Ecá tukté thípi so?" They would sing, "Where was it, did you say, that they lived?" Singing this song they would search for us and bring us to the center.

   The éyapaha called out "Úpo, úpo, léchi nichó pelo," "Come, come, they bid you to come, over here, come over here." All those who had gone through a similar ceremony were called forward. I sat in a special place of honor, and some who came forward joined me. Mom-mah noticed immediately how few there were in the center, for even then these ways were disappearing.

   "Húȟlala eháni, k'eš tóhani óta héchųšni," even in the old days, this ceremony was not done for all girls, only those whose parents could afford to do so.

Those who were cherished and for whom good things were expected. In the old days, they would have painted the part in my hair red, to show that I had the Buffalo Ceremony done for me. When I went out among the people, I would paint myself this way, to signify that I was a Buffalo Woman.

So it was, "eyá, héchųs'e maglú'onihạpi," it was the way they honored me. "Héchųs'e micíyuštạ na hehạ́l wachípi," they finished the ceremony and they enjoyed themselves dancing. "Wįmáyạ ináwažį́ héhạ . . . wawáyạkaš óta," it was then that I stood as a young Buffalo Woman in the center for all to see. I know my mother and father gave all they had, and more, to honor me that day.

Old Woman's Begging Song

Wakhályapi	Coffee
wachį́ ye	I want
aǧúyapi	bread
wachį́ ye	I want

27

Mata, A Cheyenne Woman

"Hųká eyá kį hé bluhá wą héhą," this ceremony that they call the Hųká Lowápi, or Making a Relative Ceremony, when I had it, it was done this way. It happened after the Išnáthi Awíchalową, the song they sing for one who lives alone, the ceremony for a young girl when she becomes a woman. I had it when I experienced my first menses, and after I had the Thatháka Lowápi Wó'echų, or Buffalo Ceremony.

The Hųká Lowápi is a ceremony called "making of the relatives song." It is literally that, I made a relative on the day that the ceremony was done for me. It is one of three ceremonies that a young girl could have. The first is the Išnáthi Awíchalową, the second is the Thatháka Lowápi, or Buffalo Ceremony, and the third is the Hųká Lowápi, or the Making of Relatives Ceremony. It was not necessary to do all three, but to have all three was an honor for any young girl. It meant among other things that I could paint the part in my hair red to signify that I was a Buffalo Woman. If I also had the Hųká ceremony, I could paint a red stripe across my forehead. This was the way it was done in the old days. When I wore this red paint I had to abide by certain customs requiring that I live a good moral life, or I would be punished by the spirits.

My mother and father told me it was time for me to have a "wáchįhį," an eagle plume, tied to my hair. It took them days to prepare for it. "Winúȟcala wą," an old woman, the poorest of all, was brought to the center of the "owáchi miméla," the old dance hall. They said she would do this for me. She stood in the center where she was summoned. Her name was Mata, a "Šahíyela wíyą," a woman from the Cheyenne tribe. The word "Šahíyela" identifies a people that are our allies, our friends. Mata's last name was Wąblí Núpa, or Two Eagles.

She married into our tribe as a young woman, and she lived among us, speaking Lakota as easily as she spoke Šahíyela, her own language.

She looked different from the other women who were gathered there. They wore colorful blankets draped over their shoulders, like the buffalo robes they wore in the old days. "Hé sabsápa há į na," Mata wore a thin black sackcloth shawl draped over her thin shoulders. The other women wore printed cotton cloth dresses made of colorful calico material. These long dresses reached down to cover cloth leggings and moccasins. Mata wore a black cloth dress without leggings, and she had on worn moccasins. The other women, including my mother, wore their long hair in two neat braids. Mata wore her short hair, unbound, in a blunt cut, unbecoming for any woman.

Mata was a "wiwázica," a widow. She wore black clothing because she was a widow. She didn't wear leggings because she had cut her legs to show that she was in mourning. She had slash marks on her legs for all the people to see. It was one of the only times a woman could show her legs. It was customary to scar yourself to show you were lamenting the loss of your husband. Mata followed age-old customs among the Lakotas. Her hair was cut short because she was in mourning. She put her hair in her husband's coffin so that he would recognize her when she made her journey to the spirit world. All these things indicated that she was a widow and in mourning.

They brought her to the center of the circle first, then they came for me and stood me next to her. "Él ahímagnakaha," they brought a chair to the center, and on it they draped a beautiful blanket and told me to sit on the covered chair. They gave her a "wáchįhį," a special hair ornament with a soft eagle plume hanging from it. She took it and tied it to my hair.

So it was, I stood in the center with her, that old woman, the poorest of the poor, and me, a young girl whose parents were considered able and wealthy. Her life was almost done, mine was just beginning. I was a young girl then and did not fully understand why they choose Mata. She appeared strange to me, the way she looked, but I recognized the importance of what they were doing. I knew from that time forward I would be a relative to her, and I was.

It was after Turtle Lung Woman died that my mother and father felt my sense of loss and decided to give me a new grandmother. "Hé kaȟníǧapi," they selected Mata, who had also suffered a recent loss.

When Mata tied the eagle plume to my hair, from that time forward we were related. It was the way it had to be when the Hųká ceremony was performed: "hųká," meaning "a close relative," like a mother, father, grandmother, grandfather, brother, or sister. Mata was to be my grandmother. A Cheyenne woman whose language and ways I did not fully know or understand would now be my grandmother.

"Thiwáhe kį hél ųkte škhe," now my family and household were her own. It was the way it was supposed to be when a Hųká was made. The ceremony was brought by the White Buffalo Calf Woman. When she brought the Chąnúpa Wakȟá, the Sacred Pipe, she taught our people how to live a certain way. She showed us many things, and one was how to make a Hųká. She taught us how to adopt, as relatives, among others, people who could no longer provide for themselves, so that our people may live. A hųká could be anyone, but in my case it was a Cheyenne woman who became my ųcí, my grandmother.

When she tied the eagle plume to my hair, my parents gave her many gifts. "Šúkawakhą wą, makhícima wą égleyį na ų wáchįhį imáchiya škhe," they stood a young horse in the center, as well as other things they gave to her for what she did for me. My father was especially proud to give her a "šųgmákhicima," a young horse. A Lakota man like my father honors another by giving away his most valued possession, a horse. A young horse was especially valuable and bestowed honor on the individual receiving it.

They did not just honor her in that one event, they brought her into our family, and from that time forward she was to be a part of our family. "Wótakuye," that is, they made her a relative. "Thimá icúpi," so it was "they brought it into" our large "thiyóšpaye," our extended family, that way, "thimá," the way Turtle Lung Woman used it. It was done because Mata "iháǥkeya ų́šika cha," she was the poorest of the poor, and my parents thought I needed a grandmother after Turtle Lung Woman died.

In the old days a "wó'echų" called a Huǥká Lowáǥpi, a ceremony similar to what we did in adopting Mata into our family, was done. A decorated stick was used to wave over the person's head. By the time I was growing up I only saw bits and pieces of these ceremonies because it was against the law to practice many of the old ceremonies.

What I knew was done in the "owáchi miméla," the old round dance hall, near Porcupine Creek. There, where it was not so apparent that a ceremony was being done, in that place where everyone came merely to dance. "Lé Huǥká eyá kį hé bluhá wą héha winų́hcala wą hé sabsápa há į́ áya," it was then that the old woman dressed in black became my huǥká. They showed us to all the people gathered there. "Kichí chokáta mapázopi," they took us both to the center and honored us in the circle for all the people to see.

I remember the morning after the Huǥká ceremony. There was a commotion near Mata's camp. The "šųgmáǥhicima," the young horse my father gave to Mata was killed.

"Táku echúǥpi he?" my father wanted to know what happened. "Yearling wą wichák'upi, hé kat'ápi," my mother replied, "The young yearling horse we gave to them, they killed it."

"Áta t'ehówaye, eyápi," a loud cry went up among my father and brothers. A horse, especially a good young horse like the one we gave to Mata, was considered quite valuable among the Lakotas. "How could they do something like that?" my father wondered aloud.

"Áta phátapi," my mother said, "They butchered it." She used the word "phátapi," the way we refer to the cow that they killed for the Huǥká feast. She said Mata and her immediate family were busy that morning.

My father was angry, "Tókhinaš hé yuhákte séca yų́kha wicháwak'u," he said, "I thought they were going to raise that young horse, that is why I gave it to them." He thought it senseless to kill the young horse.

What we did not know was that the Cheyennes, although they were our allies and friends since anyone could remember, were a different people than us. We, who called the horse "šúkawakhą," or "sacred dog," we would never think of killing one. But the Cheyenne did. "Héhąni hécha, Šahíyela hená šúkawakhą yútapi škhe," in those days it was said the Cheyenne ate horseflesh. They ate it as a delicacy.

"Kat'ápi na yútapi," they butchered it and ate it, the way we Lakotas enjoyed the fresh beef. A short while later my mother left and went to see Mata. When she returned, much to my father's dismay, she brought some of the horse flesh with her.

"Thaló hąké waksá yuhá. Hé icú na flour icáhi che'úpi na etą šna gluté," she took a choice piece of the flesh and rolled it in flour and fried it. When it looked like it was fully cooked, much to my father's consternation, she ate it. She considered herself a relative to Mata and did as the Cheyenne would.

A Bear Said This

Phežúta wą   A medicine root
yátįkte   you will eat
kahą́tu   at that place
nážįye   it stands
mathó   a bear
hemákiye   said to me

28

"Phežúta," Peyote

In the winter when the ceremony began it was dark. In the summer they sat down at dusk, "kítąla ápa chą," when it was still light out. We called them "meetings." The meetings were held in someone's home, usually in a room large enough to allow twenty or so people in, including children. The house was usually selected in advance, and sometimes the same house was used over and over. All of the furniture was removed from the room. Everyone brought their own blankets to sit on, or for the children to sleep on. The windows were covered with quilts and blankets, and the doors closed until daybreak, when the meeting was over.

When the ceremony began there were usually two men who ran it together, one prayed the other sang. They shared a drum, and "akíciphapi," each beat the drum for the other. They sang four songs all night long. "Okáwįȟ ú," it came in a circle so that everyone participated. The singing continued until "hąchókąyą chą," or when night was half over, when they stopped for a while.

When they stopped at midnight, someone would speak or someone would pray. So it went, and the ceremony continued. They began again, and it continued. The men continued drumming and singing. The women did not drum or sing. If children came in with their parents, they were usually asleep. So the ceremony continued with the drumming and singing. "Yé na . . . Yé na . . ." "On and on" it went.

The "phežúta," or "peyote," was passed around during the ceremony. Not everyone was required to partake of it. If you did not want it, you passed it to the person next to you.

At daybreak, "ápo chą́na šna," when the first light appeared, they prayed again. At that time they had a ceremony that is called Wanáǧi Wa'ékignaka, or "setting things out for the spirits." It was something they did only at daybreak, although it was not always necessary to do this part of the ceremony. When they did, it meant that only four things were put out for the spirits. They prepared in advance three types of "wasná," or "pemmican." There was "pápa sáka," dried meat pemmican; "wagméza," corn pemmican; and finally "chaphá," dried chokecherry pemmican. The fourth item was always "mní," water.

The water was brought in by a woman who prayed with it. Water is life. These four things were blessed, for it was believed that at daybreak the "wanáǧi" roamed the earth and the spirit food was for them. The person who blessed them, "phéta ektá ináži," would stand near the fire and take from each bowl containing one of the four foods. Once the spirit food was set out, everyone in the ceremony would take from the bowls as they were passed around and partake of the food. We believed that if we took and ate the food prepared for the spirits, we gained strength from it, so we ate it too. With it "hóyekiyapi," we sent a voice to the Creator when we offered it to the spirits.

Now then, I will say, one day, on a given day, when I was seventeen years old, I ate a lot of it, the phežúta. I ate a lot of the peyote, and I also drank a lot of peyote tea. As I was sitting there, while they were singing the songs, I suddenly blacked out. "Ųgnálaka tókhamaȟ'a," that is, without warning it was as if I disappeared. I was gone.

I felt like I was dreaming, and in that dream I saw a "pahá," a hill. On that hill, "tuwéni tukténi ųšni cha," there was no one in sight. I walked toward the hill, "wakátakiya blé," and as I walked it seemed that I was climbing upward.

I would alternate between walking and resting. I would climb for a while and then I would rest. "Ókša éwatuwa kheš áta tákunišni," I looked everywhere but there was nothing. It seemed like the only thing to do was to keep climbing. I continued walking but it seemed like a long time. It seemed like I traveled a great distance.

"Tuktógnawakhiya niš tókhiyatąhą wa'í niš táku slolwákiyešni," I did not know which way I could leave this dream, where it was I came from, and where it was I was going. I knew nothing.

I didn't give up. I just kept going. Finally, while I was resting, "ųgnálaka iblúkcą," I suddenly had a thought. "Hą, lé peyote meeting yuhá na hetą́ lé wahí." "Yes," I thought, "it was from the peyote meeting that I came here." It was then that I began to remember where it was I came from and what must have happened to me. "Iyúkcą makáhe," so I sat for a while and I thought about it.

It was then that I heard the peyote drum, its rhythm quick and uplifting. "Tah tah tah tah . . ." I could hear the hollow rapid beat of the peyote drum. I heard the sound of the rattle as well and thought I could see the man shaking it during the song. I could hear the voices of the men singing, "Hi ya na wi hi ne . . . ho ya na hi . . ." So, I stood up and began climbing again. "Ha na yo . . . ha na yo," the man sang. When I heard the singing, each time I heard the voice, I would start up again. "Phíya ibláble," I began again to climb the hill.

"Tóhą blé kį ísam naku amní, na, ųgnáhela nawaȟ'ų yúkhą," as I continued my journey I listened intently for the singing to keep myself from getting lost again. Suddenly I heard them clearly, the drum, the rattle, and the men singing. The drumming rhythm rising to a crescendo, it helped me find my way back.

When I came to, I was in the center. "Peyote hél chokáta altar s'e khiglípi, yúkhą él maké," there I was at the altar they had made in the center as they do in peyote meetings. Somehow I had crawled there. "Él ektá sloȟą́ iwáhųni," I reached the altar by crawling to it. It was through sheer will that I had crawled there. It was then that I finally heard the singing and drumming and knew fully where I was. I distinctly heard the men sing, "Ya na hi yo, wi chi na we hi yo, hi ya na, hi ye." I did not know the meaning of the words, but the song was a peyote song, one that I heard many times.

I had thought that "makhá thą́ka omáwani," I had traveled a great distance. I felt like I had returned from a great journey but in fact I had lain for two days like I was dead. It was said that another meeting had started the night I came to because I had been lying like I was dead all that day. "Akhé phíya íyotakapi na," they had sat down again to pray, but I came back into their midst at 9:00 P.M. the second night. By then, "cha echél iyémaya," I was myself again. I was well again.

This pheẑúta, this medicine that I speak of, my father and mother knew it, they used it. My mother was ill and with it was cured, "hé'ụ ząní," she was well with it. So it was, all of us, her children, came to it and attended the ceremonies, and we became members of the Native American Church.

The peyote itself was not mixed with anything. "Tákuni icáhiya na tuwéni k'úpišni," they did not put anything into it and give it to anyone. It came from Old Mexico. It grows there and is harvested and dried. They bring it back and bless it. They pray with it, use it, and gain self-knowledge with it. "Ụ waslólkhiya," that is, they understood themselves with it.

I too, believed in it, "héchụs'e wó'echelya bluhá." There were things that were distinctly Lakota, our customs that were practiced during the ceremony, that is, "Lakhóta wichówicaǧa éyạke." We were not allowed to openly practice the old religion and rituals, but these meetings were private and occurred at night.

For many winters we participated in the ceremonies, but then my mother died in one of the ceremonies. She was diabetic and went into a coma. Perhaps she went on a journey as I had but did not find her way back. By then she was in her late fifties and not as strong as I was when I willed myself home.

It seemed like a circle ended, we came to it because it healed my mother, and we left it because my mother died there. When my mother died I stayed away from many things. This ceremony was one of them. It was not that I stopped believing in it, I just stayed away from it. "Táku óta ȟeyáb ináwaẑị, hé waẑị̃," there were many things I stood away from. That was one of them. "Tuwéni éna wachį́wayešni," there was no other female I could depend on like my mother. She was gone. She left me as my grandmother Turtle Lung Woman had.

Courting Song

Ecá
wi'óbluspa yṹkhą
šṹkawakhą niníca
emákiya
cha
makhá sitómni
omáwani ye

I went
to court
a woman
but she said to me
"You have no horses"
so in sadness
I roam
the land

29

"Thawícuku," Marriage

My oldest brother's Lakota name was Zįtkála Ská, White Bird. He brought home a young woman to meet my mother and father. Her name was Jessie Ghost Bear. She was from the Sand Hills area, where the Ghost Bears lived. He wanted her to be his wife. Since he was "thokápha," the eldest, he was the honored son. "Glu'ónihapi," we say, "they treated him with great respect."

Zįtkála Ská and Jessie were to be married in an honorable way. My mother and father did not want them to stay together until they were married. "Wácag kichí ukíyapišni," that is, they did not make him stay with her right away.

Jessie was a graduate of Genoa High School. She seemed like an honorable young woman. My brother finished his schooling at the government boarding school. They seemed well suited for each other.

They were to be married at Owákpamni, or Pine Ridge, at the Holy Cross Episcopal Church. It is located at the edge of town on the road leading to White Clay. In those days the church had plenty of space around it for camping, so we gathered our tent and things we needed and started out for Owákpamni on the appointed day.

We started out in a wagon pulled by a team of horses. We left Phahí Sįté, Porcupine, in the morning and reached Pine Ridge in the early afternoon. We camped there at Holy Cross Church just as we did for important meetings, like the Convocation. We were Episcopalians because my mother liked that church. Their prayer books and hymnals were written in Lakota. Years later, Zįtkála Ská played the organ at the church in Phahí Sįté. He could read the wašícu music in the hymnals and the lyrics in Lakota.

Jessie's grandmother came and camped there, too. Jessie's mother died, and she lived with her grandmother. Her grandmother and others from her family came to the wedding. They agreed to the marriage and were happy with her choice of spouse.

In the morning they were married. The Episcopal priest performed the ceremony. My mother, father, and Jessie's grandmother put together a feast after the wedding. Once they were married, they were allowed to camp together, and that second night we all camped on the church grounds. "Kichíthi," that is, "they lived together" thereafter.

My father brought all the things Zįtkála Ská had accumulated to begin his new life as a married man. The things he needed for his household. We brought those things, including the tent they camped in after they were married and a wagon and a team of horses.

In the morning, on the third day, we all pulled up our tents and loaded our belongings. When they were ready, Zįtkála Ská and Jessie rode off together toward Nebraska, where a farmer had summoned them to work in the fields. They left in their wagon after the wedding toward White Clay and the Nebraska state line. They were married this way, "Lakhólya," or "in the Lakota way." They departed as husband and wife. We watched them leave together, and we started home toward Phahį Sįté.

A long time ago, when people were married, they brought all of their possessions to the center of the circle, where the wedding ceremony takes place. The first wedding I saw, as a child, was when Joe Fast Horse, a Lakota man, married a woman. His mother's people brought all the things he owned into the center of the circle where all the guests sat. The parents of the bride did the same. All of their possessions were in the center for all to see.

They had the man, all of his belongings, and the woman, and all of hers, in the circle. A medicine man came and blessed them. "Wakhákichiyuzapi," we say, "they were married in a sacred way." There was a feast after the wedding.

When it was over, they gathered their belongings that had been brought to the center and left together. It was the way Zįtkála Ská was married.

My brother and his wife came back for visits after that. It was Jessie, my eldest brother's wife, an educated and pretty young woman, who first impressed me enough for me to want to cut my hair. She was the first woman I saw with short hair. How I envied her even though I was a young girl.

Jessie and my eldest brother had been gone for a while, living and working in Nebraska. One day they came home, and to the astonishment of my mother and grandmother, Jessie had short hair. "Wayáwa cha héchų," everyone said, "It was because she went to school and was educated in the white way."

I do not think my mother approved or disapproved, because when I begged her to have my hair cut she let me do it too. I did not cut it right away, but when I was old enough, she let me cut it. I remember how my decision to cut my hair was an event itself. It was a call for a special ceremony. "Wó'yu'onihą él yąké," an honoring ceremony, was attached to it.

In the old days, we had certain beliefs concerning hair. When the old people like Turtle Lung Woman combed their hair they would take all the fallen hair on the comb, roll it up, and throw it into the fire. They never left hair on the ground or anywhere other than on their own persons because they believed that someone could take another person's hair and gain power over them in some bad way.

One of my sisters-in-law never cut her hair to the day she died in her eighty-fourth year. Her name was Lucille Her Horse, she married my second-eldest brother. She was like my sister. She came home with my brother in 1929, when she was fifteen years old, and she stayed. She never returned to her own people even after my brother died. Her maiden name is Šųgléwį, or Her Horse. She is from Hisle, near the town of Wanblee. My brother went there to see her and brought her home to be his wife. She came riding home on a horse that belonged to my brother. She stayed. I had no other sisters, only five brothers, and some of my sisters-in-law became like real sisters to me. She was one of them.

30

Brooks Horse

I went to school until I was eighteen. Then I was married and I stopped going to school. The man I married was a "khoškálaka," a young man who owned many things. He owned many acres of land. I was married for three years when he left me.

He had been working in the Conservation Corps in Hill City, South Dakota, when we met in 1938. He wrote to me and I wrote back. He came to see me, and I liked his quiet mannerisms. I was not a quiet woman, even then I was outspoken.

I was married in the Catholic Church. My mother-in-law insisted that we be married in the Catholic Church. She said her family was Catholic and would not accept that my family was Episcopalian. So, Brooks and I were married at the Catholic church. It was not until later that I found out that Brooks was not a Catholic but an Episcopalian like me.

My mother and father-in-law lived in Pine Ridge, in the middle of many Catholics, and she wanted to be like them. They were mostly half-bloods or half-Lakota. She did not want anything to do with the church attended by full-bloods like my family. We went to it because it celebrated our language in its prayer books and hymnals. We could speak our language in the services. When we prayed in Lakota, in the language we spoke in our daily lives, it did not matter what denomination it was, as long as we could pray in our language.

I respected her wishes and I was married in that church I grew to dread. I had attended the Catholic boarding school for a short while. I remembered the Mass and how we had to kneel for long periods of time. I left the school when I suffered an eye injury. While I was at the school, we were taking a walk in the woods behind the school and a sharp branch poked me in the eye. My right eye was infected for a while and they sent me home. I did not go back to the boarding school after that. I stayed and attended the school near my home. I was just glad not to go back to that school.

While he was working in the Conservation Corps in Hill City, Brooks, my first husband, may have been exposed to the disease tuberculosis, which killed him at a young age. He became infected with it. When the chest pains were too much for him to bear, he went home. He did not want to give it to me.

We were living in a small house in a buffalo pasture in Allen, South Dakota. It seemed far from where I lived with my mother and father. The land was no different, the same rolling hills as where I lived most of my life. I did not feel lonely, as long as my young husband stayed with me.

We had a little girl, Jessica, by then. He did not want to infect her so he went home to be with his mother and father. When I first became pregnant with our daughter, I enjoyed my husband's concern and attention. He took me for long walks up the dirt road from our house. He said it would be better for me to stay active, so we walked on quiet evenings.

When our daughter Jessica was born, I remember her dark, thick hair. She was born with black hair that was matted to her head. How she cried, "ah un, ah un," it sounded like a small insignificant cry in that large buffalo pasture in Allen. I put a small bonnet on her head and tied it tight. In the old days, I would have made a small cap sown out of the softest buckskin to put on her head. It is to keep her warm and to protect the soft spot on her skull. I was always afraid that she would catch a chill. I did not want to undress her to bathe her, afraid that she would get sick from the draft or cold. I kept her carefully bundled in layers of blankets.

When the disease began to show itself, Brooks could no longer walk for any distance. He was short of breath and finally caught pneumonia. It was then that he went home to his family. He left us and went home to live with his mother and father in Pine Ridge.

I was alone there with my young daughter, Jessica. My father sent my brothers to check on me. Soon after he left, I followed Brooks to Pine Ridge. I knew I risked getting the disease, but I wanted to be with him. When Brooks died of the disease, I went home and lived there with my daughter. I felt alone, but that was the way I lived.

When the men worked in the fields in Nebraska, around the year 1941, I joined them at potato picking time and corn picking time. I worked in the fields along with the other women. "Owápha," I joined in. I was twenty-one years old and able to do the things they did.

I grew stronger working in the fields after Brooks died. Those cold mornings in September and October, I stood among the older women while they warmed themselves near an open fire at the end of the field. I thought about my young husband, Brooks Horse. How he, too, knew hard work. His hands were slender and callused. How he would never hold his daughter again.

I thought about us, what I would be doing if Brooks were alive. I know we would have followed my family into the fields. I know he would have worked hard for Jessica and me. He left many acres of land for us. I inherited what he owned. It helped me stay independent for a long time. Zįtkála Ská, my older brother, would sell it little by little for me. Eventually I sold all the land that Brooks left for me.

I did not know then that my young husband had infected our infant daughter. She died a short while after he did. Jessica is buried at St. Julia's Church, where Turtle Lung Woman and my grandfather Bear Goes in the Wood are buried. I have been there many times since to bury many relatives. In 1941, when Brooks and Jessica died, I was twenty-one years old, my adult life as a married woman and mother ended abruptly. I went home and was alone again. "Iwáhables'e," it was as if I had dreamed of a life as a woman in a buffalo pasture in Allen.

Epilogue

My mother, Wíya Išnála, Turtle Lung Woman's granddaughter, lived for another fifty-eight years beyond this story. After Jessica died in 1941, she gave birth to nine children between the years 1943 and 1961. This story ends in 1941 because that is the time period she chose to share with me.

On March 27, 1999, I traveled to a hospital located off the reservation to see my mother. I spent the night in her room. I woke up at 6:00 A.M., lying in a roll-away bed in a corner by a window. I showered and dressed and sat down to watch the night nurse attend to her before she left her shift. On that day, March 28, 1999, at 7:15 A.M., according to the night nurse's notes in her chart, Wíya Išnála's heart stopped.

Immediately after her heart stopped, I held her warm, soft hand. The top of her hands were scarred from too many needles being put into them at the two hospitals she had been in. Her hands were worn from the labor she had seen in her day. I had seen her wash clothes in a metal bucket with a washboard when I was small. Those hands rubbing the clothes up and down on the washboard. I had seen her kneading bread with those hands. Her sure way of throwing the dough back and forth before she put it in the oven. I had admired the way her hands could break an apple in half, they were so strong. How crisp the apple sounded when it yielded to her strong fingers.

I remembered so much as I held her hands. My own life merged with hers in one brief moment. I did not want to let her hands go. I did not want to grow up. I wanted to remain her daughter. I knew then what she meant when she said, "Úye imáyapi," "They left me behind," meaning those who passed on to the spirit world.

As she lay in her room that bright Sunday morning, a man brought some drummers and a group of singers. They sang Sun Dance songs in her room, calling out her name, Wíyą Išnála. My heart was heavy, but I thought I saw a vision of her walking away, to the north, among the pine. Wazíyata, where the Lakota spirit world is. How strong she looked. When the drummers finished her song, she kept walking. She didn't look back but walked over the hill. She walked through the buffalo grass. I saw how good the winds were that blew around her and through the grass. She said a medicine man had told her she would live to see the "phežíša," or "red grass," in the early springtime.

I held her hands days later when she lay in her coffin, when they were as cold as ice, her strong Lakota profile forever chiseled in my mind. Her spirit hovered those next few days. I know she was with me. She left me the daunting task of burying her. I did it the best I could, but in the end I was a coward.

At her gravesite I looked up the hillside and remembered how she had last told me she would show me the grave of Mathó Chą Wígni Iyá, Bear Goes in the Wood. There it stood, on top of the hillside. I walked up to it and walked around it, as if I would see some sign of them, Mathó Chą Wígni Iyá, Kheglézela Chaǧúwį, and Wíyą Išnála, my mother. I did not see them that day. I only heard the horses in the valley to the north call out and the horses near where I stood answer.

I remember an old song: "Wakhákhąyą wa'ų, maȟpíyata wákhita yé, wakhákhąyą wa'ų, mitháš̌uke óta ye." It goes like this: "In a sacred manner I live, to the sky I implore, in a sacred manner, I live. My horses are many because I live this way."

That day when I said goodbye, at the hospital, Wíyą Išnála's hands were still warm. "Tókša akhé wąchíyąkįkte ephé," I told her, "I will see you again."

In the American Indian Lives series

First to Fight
By Henry Mihesuah
Edited by Devon Abbott Mihesuah

Mourning Dove
A Salishan Autobiography
Edited by Jay Miller

I'll Go and Do More
Annie Dodge Wauneka,
Navajo Leader and Activist
By Carolyn Niethammer

John Rollin Ridge
His Life and Works
By James W. Parins

Singing an Indian Song
A Biography of D'Arcy McNickle
By Dorothy R. Parker

Crashing Thunder
The Autobiography of an
American Indian
Edited by Paul Radin

Turtle Lung Woman's
Granddaughter
By Delphine Red Shirt
and Lone Woman

Telling a Good One
The Process of a Native American
Collaborative Biography
By Theodore Rios and
Kathleen Mullen Sands

Sacred Feathers
The Reverend Peter Jones
(Kahkewaquonaby) and the
Mississauga Indians
By Donald B. Smith

Grandmother's Grandchild
My Crow Indian Life
By Alma Hogan Snell
Edited by Becky Matthews
Foreword by Peter Nabokov

Blue Jacket
Warrior of the Shawnees
By John Sugden

I Tell You Now
Autobiographical Essays by
Native American Writers
Edited by Brian Swann and
Arnold Krupat

Postindian Conversations
By Gerald Vizenor and A. Robert Lee

Chainbreaker
The Revolutionary War Memoirs of
Governor Blacksnake
As told to Benjamin Williams
Edited by Thomas S. Abler

Standing in the Light
A Lakota Way of Seeing
By Severt Young Bear and R. D. Theisz

Sarah Winnemucca
By Sally Zanjani